Occupational Safety and Health Act of 1970

"To assure safe and healthful working conditions for working men and women; by authorizing enforcement of the standards developed under the Act; by assisting and encouraging the States in their efforts to assure safe and healthful working conditions; by providing for research, information, education, and training in the field of occupational safety and health."

This publication provides a general overview of a particular standards-related topic. This publication does not alter or determine compliance responsibilities which are set forth in OSHA standards, and the *Occupational Safety and Health Act*. Moreover, because interpretations and enforcement policy may change over time, for additional guidance on OSHA compliance requirements, the reader should consult current administrative interpretations and decisions by the Occupational Safety and Health Review Commission and the courts.

This information will be made available to sensory impaired individuals upon request. Voice phone: (202) 693-1999; teletypewriter (TTY) number: 1-877-889-5627.

Best Practices for Protecting EMS Responders
during Treatment and Transport of Victims of Hazardous Substance Releases

Occupational Safety and Health Administration
U.S. Department of Labor

OSHA 3370-11
2009

Cover photo courtesy of Dr. John Hick

Acknowledgements

Numerous individuals, agencies and organizations assisted in the development of this publication. OSHA wishes to express its deepest appreciation to the following for their significant contributions to this guide.

American Ambulance Association

American Medical Response

Agency for Toxic Substances and Disease Registry, Emergency Response

Boston Emergency Medical Services

Department of Homeland Security, Federal Emergency Management Agency, National Emergency Training Center

Emergency Nurses Association

EnMagine, Inc.

Hennepin County Medical Center, Dept of Emergency Medicine

Elsevier Public Safety, Journal of Emergency Medical Services

National Association of EMS Educators

National Association of EMS Physicians

National Institute for Occupational Safety and Health

New York City Fire Department

North Shore – LIJ Health System, Center for Emergency Medical Services, Special Operations Division

Objective Safety, LLC

U.S. Department of Health and Human Services

U.S. Department of Transportation

U.S. Environmental Protection Agency

The following agencies and organizations reviewed and provided comments:

Emergency Nurses Association

EnMagine, Inc.

Hennepin County Medical Center, Department of Emergency Medicine

National Association of EMS Educators

National Association of EMS Physicians

National Association of State EMS Officials

National Institute for Occupational Safety and Health, Emergency Preparedness and Response Coordination Office

New Jersey Department of Health and Senior Services, Division of Epidemiology Environmental and Occupational Health

New York City Fire Department, Office of Medical Affairs

National Institutes of Health/National Institute of Environmental Health Sciences, Worker Education Training Branch

North Shore – LIJ Health System, Center for Emergency Medical Services

Objective Safety, LLC

U.S. Agency for Toxic Substances and Disease Registry, Emergency Response

U.S. Department of Homeland Security, Federal Emergency Management Agency

U.S. Department of Health and Human Services

U.S. Department of Transportation

OSHA®
Occupational Safety and
Health Administration

Contents

Acronyms

APF	Assigned protection factor	**HSEES**	Hazardous Substances Emergency Events Surveillance
APR	Air-purifying respirator	**HVA**	Hazard vulnerability analysis
ASR	Atmosphere supplying respirator	**IDLH**	Immediately dangerous to life or health
ATSDR	Agency for Toxic Substances and Disease Registry	**ICS**	Incident command system
CBRN	Chemical, biological, radiological, or nuclear [agent or substance]	**IC**	Incident commander
CBRNE	Chemical, biological, radiological, nuclear, or explosive [agent or substance]	**JCAHO**	Joint Commission on Accreditation of Healthcare Organizations
CDC	Centers for Disease Control and Prevention	**LEPC**	Local emergency planning committee
CERCLA	Comprehensive Environmental Response, Compensation, and Liability Act	**LERP**	Local emergency response plan
		NFPA	National Fire Protection Association
CFR	Code of Federal Regulation	**NHTSA**	National Highway Traffic Safety Administration
EMS	Emergency Medical Services	**NIOSH**	National Institute for Occupational Safety and Health
EMT	Emergency medical technicians [of all levels]	**NIMS**	The National Incident Management System
ERP	Emergency response plan	**NRC**	Nuclear Regulatory Commission
HAZCOM	Hazard Communication (29 CFR 1910.120)	**PPE**	Personal protective equipment
HAZMAT	Hazardous material	**PAPR**	Powered air-purifying respirator
HAZWOPER	Hazardous Waste Operations and Emergency Response (29 CFR 1910.120)	**SCBA**	Self-contained breathing apparatus
		SAR	Supplied-air respirator
HEPA	High efficiency particulate air [filtration system]	**SERP**	State emergency response plan
		TB	Tuberculosis
HICS	Hospital Incident Command System	**TSCA**	Toxic Substances Control Act of 1976

See Appendix A for glossary of terms

OSHA®
Occupational Safety and Health Administration

Executive Summary

In 2005, OSHA published the *Best Practices for Hospital-Based First Receivers* guide that provided guidance for those healthcare facilities that receive and treat victims of hazardous substance releases. At the request of stakeholders that participated in the development of that guide, OSHA has developed a similar guide for emergency medical service (EMS) responders who provide medical assistance during an incident involving a hazardous substance release. This guide is intended for employers of EMS responders and discusses the measures these employers need to take to protect their EMS responders from becoming additional victims while on the front line of medical response.

Scope

EMS responders are broadly defined here as the individuals who provide pre-hospital emergency medical care and patient transportation. Some EMS responders are also assigned duties that support patient care, including patient decontamination. For the purpose of this guide, the term *EMS responder* refers to all levels of emergency medical personnel involved in incident response (e.g., emergency medical technicians [EMTs], paramedics, and others who perform similar duties). While many EMS responders are cross-trained (e.g., EMT and firefighter), this guide applies to these workers only when they are functioning as EMS responders.

The Employer's Role

Preplanning helps employers ensure that their workers have adequate training and personal protective equipment (PPE) for the incidents in which the workers are expected to participate. Critical steps for the employer involve determining the EMS responder's expected role in a reasonably anticipated worst-case scenario, identifying the hazards that are associated with the EMS responder's assigned duties, and developing an emergency response plan (ERP) that spells out how the EMS responder will be prepared (through training and PPE) to safely fulfill those duties (OSHA Instruction CPL-02-02-073, *Emergency Responses to Hazardous Substance Releases*, Aug. 27, 2007).

OSHA's Recommendations

OSHA's recommendations on minimum training and PPE for EMS responders assisting patients at hazardous substance release sites generally follow regulatory requirements contained in paragraph (q) of OSHA's Hazardous Waste Operations and Emergency Response (HAZWOPER) standard (29 Code of Federal Regulations [CFR] 1910.120) and associated guidelines and interpretive letters. In some instances, OSHA also recommends that, as a best practice, employers consider offering instruction to certain EMS responders who would not otherwise receive HAZWOPER training under regulatory requirements, but who OSHA believes might find themselves in a situation where this training would allow them to make better decisions to protect both themselves and other EMS personnel.

Table 2 at pg. 32 of this guide summarizes these requirements and best practices for EMS responders who might be assigned to assist patients under certain situations.

For example, if an EMS responder would be assigned to provide:

* medical assistance in an environment that is potentially immediately dangerous to life and health (IDLH), whether in the hot or the warm zone, then the employer must provide HAZWOPER first responder operations level training, a self-contained breathing apparatus (SCBA) as respiratory protection and Level A or Level B PPE, in accordance with OSHA requirements (29 CFR 1910.120(q)(3)(iv) and Appendix B of that standard). This level of protection may be modified by the incident commander (IC) as information becomes available. By definition, activities such as treating contaminated patients and decontaminating patients occur in the warm zone. The hot, warm, and cold zones are defined in Appendix A.

* medical assistance only in the cold zone, assisting uncontaminated or thoroughly decontaminated patients during a hazardous substance release event, then OSHA strongly recommends that, as a minimum, employers provide HAZWOPER first responder awareness level training. OSHA also suggests that the next higher level of HAZWOPER training, first responder operations level, be provided to these workers as an appropriate "best practice" because of the possibility of incomplete decontamination or inaccurate triage performed by others. Regardless of the level of training, the minimum respiratory protection for workers in the cold zone would be only that needed for infection control purposes.

* emergency transport for uncontaminated patients during emergencies involving an IDLH environment or the release of an unknown/

uncharacterized hazardous substance, then OSHA strongly recommends HAZWOPER first responder awareness level training or, preferably first responder operations level training.

- uncontaminated patient transport at an incident only after the hazardous substance is adequately characterized, OSHA recommends that these workers receive hazard communication training, or as a best practice, first responder awareness level training. The minimum respiratory protection would be only that needed for infection control purposes.

- inter-facility transport only (i.e., never respond to 911 calls), then if such a worker is unexpectedly called upon to respond to an emergency involving a hazardous substance release, OSHA requires that the worker must be trained as "skilled support personnel" (29 CFR 1910.120(q)(4)). The employer should confirm that no contracts or cooperative arrangements exist that could result in workers responding to the site of an emergency involving a hazardous material. Such agreements would indicate that these duties are expected, and, therefore, the responders should be appropriately trained in advance.

Best Practices Guide Content

The first section of this guide offers employers suggestions for obtaining information that will help them determine the roles that their workers may play in an emergency response. This section also provides information to help employers assess the hazards their workers may encounter in the event of a hazardous substance release incident. This section concludes with identifying information that should be included in the ERP.

The next two sections provide best practices on training and equipping EMS responders during treatment and transport of potentially contaminated victims. Table 2 presents best practice recommendations for levels of training and PPE for EMS responders. Employers may incorporate these training and PPE levels into their ERPs, citing this best practices document as the basis for those selections.

A final section addresses hazardous substance decontamination. Although EMS responders might not be assigned to a community's decontamination team, they should understand the process if they are to recognize ineffective decontamination procedures that could result in improperly decontaminated patients – patients that EMS responders could be expected to treat and/or transport. Furthermore, OSHA believes that during a mass casualty incident, EMS responders could be assigned to assist with decontamination and would need to know how to perform effective patient decontamination.

Appendices to this guide provide supplemental information and examples related to issues raised by this guide.

> The Web site URLs cited in this document were effective as of the date of publication. Be aware that URLs are often changed. If the Web site URL does not work, go to the home page of the organization. This can usually be done by deleting all of the URL characters after the first forward slash. For instance, if the site is http://www.cdc.gov/niosh/docs/2005-100/, the home page would be located at www.cdc.gov. You may then be able to find the web page of interest by following links on the home page.

OSHA®
Occupational Safety and
Health Administration

Introduction

Emergency medical services (EMS) responders are a critical part of the nation's emergency response system and the front line of medical response. They provide medical treatment at the scene of an incident and are often among the first group of responders to arrive. As a result, EMS responders are also likely to be present on the scene before hazards are brought fully under control and before situational awareness is complete. Incident sites routinely contain evolving hazards that can harm emergency responders. This Best Practices document addresses the special conditions presented by dangerous substances released at the site of an emergency response and discusses the measures employers need to take to protect their EMS responders from becoming additional victims at sites involving hazardous substances.

This guide offers the employers of EMS responders suggestions on how to determine the roles their workers will perform in the event of a hazardous substance release incident. Employers are expected to protect their EMS responders by preparing them for their roles in hazardous substance response with appropriate training and PPE. Worker training and PPE provided should correspond, so that each EMS responder is equipped with PPE that will allow that employee to work safely in the role for which he or she is trained.

The basic steps for achieving appropriate EMS worker protection include:

1) The employer determines the EMS responder's expected role in reasonably anticipated worst-case scenarios.

2) The employer conducts a hazard assessment to identify the anticipated hazards associated with the EMS responder's role.

3) The employer develops an ERP that spells out how the EMS responder will be prepared to safely perform the responder's anticipated role. The plan should indicate the level of training that the EMS responder should receive and the type of PPE that will be provided to that responder.

This document consolidates existing OSHA policy and guidance on training and PPE for EMS responders and is intended to help EMS responders save lives without becoming additional victims.[1]

---

[1] The existing OSHA policy and guidance appear in OSHA standards and letters of interpretation cited throughout this document.

Scope and Objectives

EMS responders are broadly defined here as the individuals who provide pre-hospital emergency medical care. EMS responder activities can encompass all levels of patient emergency care, treatment, or transport provided at the incident location or between that location and the receiving hospital or other healthcare facility (i.e., inter-facility transportation). Depending on the community in which they serve, some EMS responders are also expected to assist with other related duties that support patient care, including patient decontamination.

EMS Responders: For the purposes of this document, the term EMS responder refers to all levels of emergency medical personnel involved in incident response. This group includes emergency medical technicians (EMTs) of various levels, paramedics, and others who perform the duties of an EMT or paramedic, regardless of their job title or employment status. These individuals serve as the "public's emergency medical safety net" and will continue to do so as the EMS system evolves in the future (NHTSA, 2000).[2]

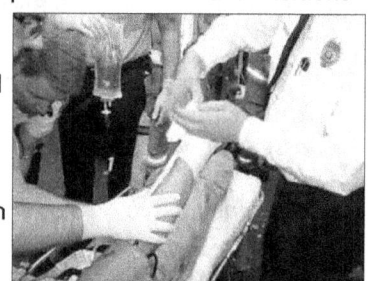

Photo courtesy of Jennifer Lyden

> These recommendations are best suited for those individuals for whom providing medical care is a primary mission. Others may benefit from these recommendations, but might also have additional training that expands their capabilities during emergencies involving hazardous materials.
>
> This best practices document is not intended to advise other responders (e.g., firefighters, police) when they perform work beyond the duties of an EMS responder.

All Workers Functioning as EMS Responders: This guide is intended for employers of EMS responders of all types. This document is equally relevant to EMS responders who are volunteers, full- or part-time workers, and personnel of agen-

---

[2] From: NHSTA, undated. EMS Education Agenda for the Future. Last accessed May 19, 2007. Available at www.nhtsa.dot.gov/people/injury/ems/EdAgenda/final/agenda600.htm#core

cies, fire departments, or hospitals while they are providing the services of an EMS responder at an incident site or during patient transport.[3] Although many EMS responders are cross-trained or hold multiple qualifications (e.g., EMT and firefighter or HAZMAT team member), OSHA considers this guide relevant to these individuals only while they are performing the duties of an EMS responder. It is not applicable when an EMS responder who is cross-trained as a firefighter or HAZMAT team member is performing work to fight a fire or "handle or control actual or potential leaks or spills of hazardous substances requiring possible close approach to the substance."

Hazardous Substance Release: Emergency response to a hazardous substance release is defined here as it is in OSHA's Hazardous Waste Operations and Emergency Response (HAZWOPER) standard:

> *"...a response effort by employees from outside the immediate release area or by other designated responders (i.e., mutual aid groups, local fire departments, etc.) to an occurrence which results, or is likely to result, in an uncontrolled release of a hazardous substance. Responses to incidental releases of hazardous substances where the substance can be absorbed, neutralized, or otherwise controlled at the time of release by employees in the immediate release area, or by maintenance personnel are not considered to be emergency responses within the scope of this [HAZWOPER] Standard. Responses to releases of hazardous substances where there is no potential safety or health hazard (i.e., fire, explosion, or chemical exposure) are not considered to be emergency responses" (29 CFR 1910.120(a)(3)).*

OSHA acknowledges the dynamic tension that exists between the need to provide expedient medical treatment (including taking patients to a site where they can receive more advanced care) and the need to protect the medical care provider.

This document focuses on reasonably anticipated worst-case scenarios with the understanding that these situations will be relatively rare. Nevertheless, the associated preparation will benefit employers and EMS responders any time patients require emergency medical assistance at the scene of a hazardous substance release.

---

[3] See Appendix P for further discussion of OSHA jurisdiction over public employees.

Hazards and Routes of Exposure: This guide specifically covers protection for EMS responders during responses to releases of chemicals, radiological particles, and biological agents that result in patients who may need emergency on-scene medical care, decontamination, and/or transportation from the scene of the release to the hospital. When such hazardous substances are present, EMS responders may become exposed to the substances through direct airborne or physical contact with the contaminant at the scene, or through secondary contact while caring for a patient who became contaminated with the substance at the scene.[4]

At the Scene of the Release: This guide focuses on protecting EMS responders who answer requests for emergency medical care at (or in close proximity to) the scene of the hazardous substance release. For this purpose, OSHA has placed an emphasis on EMS response to a release of harmful chemicals, radiological materials, or biological agents – such as an anthrax spore powder – during the initial release (i.e., when the release is discovered at the time of the incident). This document does not address cases where the scene of the release is unknown, or where the scene was identified only later through epidemiological methods, when EMS responders would no longer be required at the scene. Furthermore, this document does not cover EMS responder protections for infectious agents when a release is identified retrospectively only after the identification of sick individuals. This latter category includes infectious agents such as those causing highly pathogenic avian influenza, severe acute respiratory syndrome (SARS), plague, smallpox, or tularemia, when spread by natural, insidious, or clandestine release.[5] In these cases, OSHA recommends that employers consult CDC for

---

[4] Hazardous substance is defined as any substance exposure that may result in adverse effects on the health or safety of employees. This includes substances defined under Section 101(14) of CERCLA; biological or disease-causing agents that may reasonably be anticipated to cause death, disease, or other health problems; any substance listed by the U.S. Department of Transportation as hazardous material under 49 CFR 172.101 and appendices; and substances classified as hazardous waste. See 1910.120(a)(3).

[5] As a special case, release of an infectious disease would be covered by this document if a known intentional or accidental release occurred at a known location, so that an incident scene is recognized at the time of the release. As a rule of thumb, a key test is the question: "Would immediate surface or victim decontamination affect the course of the incident?" If the answer is "no"– because victims who were at the scene have already become infected – then CDC guidelines for handling infectious disease incidents will be more relevant than these best practices from OSHA.

OSHA®
Occupational Safety and
Health Administration

information on EMS responder protections. For a brief discussion of biological agents and a list of useful Web sites, see Appendix Q – Sources of Help in Addressing Biological Agent Issues.

Purpose

Employers of EMS responders will find this document useful during development of hazard evaluations and ERPs. The purpose of this guide is to establish best practices that EMS employers can implement to help EMS responders save lives without becoming additional victims. To this end, the document will help inform employers about:

- The relevance of OSHA's HAZWOPER standard to EMS responders.

- Methods for obtaining information on the types of hazardous substance release events that the local community is preparing to address.

- The importance of identifying responder roles and responsibilities in the community (including those under mutual aid agreements).

- Important topics to consider while developing an ERP.

- OSHA's recommendations and requirements for training and PPE when EMS responders' roles include the potential for response to incidents involving hazardous substance(s).

Organization of this Guide

OSHA's *Best Practices for Protecting EMS Responders during Treatment and Transport of Victims of Hazardous Substance Releases* is organized into seven sections, including this introduction and a brief conclusion.

The next sections provide background and support for OSHA recommendations on training and PPE (including respiratory protection) for EMS responders who could reasonably be anticipated to respond to an event involving a hazardous substance release.

A summary of training and PPE is then provided with a summary table (Table 2) to look up the recommended minimum training and PPE needed for EMS responders assigned to specific roles and under a range of anticipated conditions. Employers may cite this information when conducting hazard evaluations required by OSHA standards on respiratory protection and PPE. See Figure 1 at pg. 34 for simple instructions on using the summary table.

The final section reviews topics related to patient and responder decontamination. Although EMS responders in many communities are not routinely assigned to decontamination teams, they need to be prepared to identify improper or inadequate decontamination in patients they receive. Additionally, OSHA believes that it is naive to assume that some EMS responders would not be tasked with decontamination during an event that involves mass casualties.

This guide is supplemented with appendices that provide additional details on topics introduced in the text, including a detailed glossary and a list of the references cited throughout the document and its appendices.

Determinants of Training and PPE: Personnel Roles, Hazard Assessments and Emergency Response Plans

OSHA considers appropriate worker preparation to encompass both training and PPE. To determine necessary training and PPE, the employer must understand all workers' roles and the associated hazards. EMS responders should be adequately trained for their role in emergency response during hazardous substance events. Furthermore, each worker's training and PPE should be compatible, so that the EMS responder is equipped with PPE that will allow that individual to work safely in the role for which that he or she is trained.

The basic steps for determining necessary training and PPE include:

1) The employer determines the EMS responder's expected role in a reasonably anticipated worst-case scenario.

2) The employer conducts a hazard assessment to identify any anticipated hazards associated with the EMS responder's role during such a response.

3) The employer develops an ERP that spells out how the EMS responders will be prepared to safely perform their anticipated roles. The plan should indicate the level of training that the EMS responders should receive and the type of PPE that will be provided to those responders.

This section outlines regulations, information sources and prudent practices that shape employers' decisions about EMS responder preparation. The decisions that employers make about EMS responder roles, training and PPE should be outlined in the employers' ERPs.

EMS Responder's Role in the Community

OSHA standards and letters of interpretation require employers to tailor EMS responder training and PPE to (1) the duties that EMS responders are "expected" to perform, and (2) the expected hazards that EMS responders can reasonably be anticipated to encounter while performing those duties. Thus, both the duties and the hazards must be defined in order to reasonably establish training and protection for an EMS responder.

> If multiple persons are down (i.e., incapacitated) in a public area and there is no obvious trauma, then [a HAZWOPER trained EMS responder]

> should immediately suspect a chemical exposure or attack. EMS responders without proper PPE should never enter such an area, or if they do enter before realizing the problem, they should immediately exit while only removing those closest to the exit (OSHA Stakeholder Comments, 2006).

Specifically, in a 1991 letter of interpretation OSHA clarified that EMS personnel should be trained in accordance with the responsibilities they will be expected to assume during an emergency response as described in the community emergency response plan (OSHA, 1991-McNamara). Furthermore, OSHA's Personal Protective Equipment standard requires that the employer select appropriate PPE based on the hazards that are present, or likely to be present, including foreseeable emergencies (see Personal Protective Equipment for additional information on required written documentation associated with the PPE and respiratory protection selection processes). When specific hazards cannot be identified in advance, OSHA expects that employers will consider the reasonably anticipated *"worst-case employee exposure scenarios"* (OSHA, 2002-Hayden).

The following two sections discuss factors that employers of EMS responders should consider when evaluating their workers' roles in emergency response events and the hazards that EMS responders encounter while performing their jobs.

Defining the EMS Responder Role in Community Response: Factors to Evaluate, Contacts, Information Sources and Special Considerations

The employer is ultimately responsible for determining the duties to which individual EMS responders could be assigned. By defining workers' roles to address community expectations, the employer will be better able to anticipate how to prepare their EMS responders for these roles and any associated hazardous conditions.

As a first step toward identifying EMS responder roles, the employer should determine whether or not its workers would be made available to respond to an emergency. For some employers of EMS responders involved in 911 response this is an easy decision. Other employers might find this more dif-

ficult to answer. For instance, some employers might employ EMS responders who never respond to an emergency, but rather work as inter-facility transport EMTs, transferring patients between medical facilities. As a guideline, OSHA recommends that employers train and prepare their workers to respond to an emergency if the employers are party to existing contracts (e.g., with the county or municipality) that call for the employers to participate in emergency response in the event of a disaster. Furthermore, if employers are covered by a disaster mutual aid agreement or cooperative arrangement with other emergency services providers or communities, then the employers should prepare their workers accordingly.

Having determined that their workers might respond to an emergency, employers should find out how and under what circumstances the community expects the EMS providers to respond. This information will help employers determine the roles to which they will assign their personnel.

Photo courtesy of Frank Califano

"The emergency response plan for the jurisdiction should clearly define who will be responsible for decontaminating victims during an emergency response. The emergency medical service personnel should be trained in accordance with the responsibilities they will be expected to assume during an emergency response as described in the community emergency response plan." (OSHA, 1991-McNamara).

Employers of EMS responders can easily describe their workers' day-to-day duties, but they might find it more difficult to anticipate the actions and hazards associated with EMS responder duties in the event of a mass casualty event, in the face of a new threat, or during a large-scale disaster involving several communities. These roles are typically based on community emergency response plan-

ners' decisions, which are in part based upon perceived risks, resources, availability of other responders, and to some extent, the influence or perceptions of the broader community (e.g., citizens, businesses, news media).

By understanding the needs and expectations of community leaders, emergency planners, other responders, and typical citizens, employers can better anticipate how and where they may be asked to engage their workers under various emergency circumstances.

The expectations of the community (as expressed by its emergency planners) may be assessed from several perspectives:

- What role does the community expect an individual EMS service provider to fill?

- What actions and tasks does the community expect EMS responders to fill?

- Under what circumstances will these responsibilities be performed?

- Where within the continuum of hazard response zones does the community expect EMS responders to respond?

- What actions does the community expect the EMS responder to take when they encounter contaminated patients?

- Does the community provide detection equipment and expect EMS responders to use it (e.g., ionizing radiation detectors, chemical detectors)?

- How many EMS responders, if any, need to be prepared to function in the most dangerous areas (e.g., the hot zone) compared to the numbers of EMS responders needed in areas with reduced or no potential for hazardous substance exposure? Are an adequate number of properly trained and equipped fire- or HAZMAT-team based EMS responders available to fill this need?

Photo courtesy of Jennifer Lyden

- What additional training is required to prepare EMS responders to meet possible situations they could encounter during emergency response?

- Who will treat patients in the warm zone?

Specifically, the EMS employer should work with the local emergency management agency, Local Emergency Planning Committee (LEPC), fire department, HAZMAT team, police, and other response partners consistent with the state and local government structure, to determine:

- Who will be performing decontamination activities and to what extent?

- Who will remove victims from the hot zone?

- Who will treat victims trapped in a dangerous area?[6]

- Who will transport patients removed from the scene once first responders assess them?

- Who will be available as backup, if needed?

As an additional step, it is important to work with the community to define expectations of where in the danger continuum (from release site to a safe and clean area) the EMS responders could perform their designated tasks.

Unless they have addressed these questions in advance with the community, employers of EMS responders will find themselves making difficult decisions at the last minute under emergency conditions. Undefined or unwritten expectations can hinder EMS providers' ability to make good decisions and might result in responders arriving on the scene unprepared or poorly equipped.

> "Whatever roles are chosen, it should be clear that SOME agency in the community has the responsibility and training to provide patient care in the warm zone (at least) and is properly equipped to do so. This could be an issue if the community has a fire department without medical responsibilities/training and they are the only ones with Level B PPE." (OSHA Stakeholder Comments, 2006).

The Value of Open Dialogue

Community planners should ensure that EMS responders participate in discussions of emergency preparedness and exercises involving mutual aid. The better the community's organizations and its citizens understanding of the strengths and limita-

tions of their EMS system, the more realistic the community's expectations will be during an actual emergency. Additionally, employers that foster open and trusting dialogue between themselves and these community groups during day-to-day operations will find it easier to share valuable information in times of crisis. In the midst of a disaster, that shared information might help remind community members of both the greatest strengths and the realistic limitations of their EMS responders. This could help protect employers from being pressured by the demands of unrealistic community expectations into providing EMS responders for activities for which they are not properly trained or equipped.

> Background information for media might include answers to:
> - Why are some responders equipped and trained to one level, while others are prepared at a different level? How does this benefit the community?
> - What are the benefits and limitations of different types of protective equipment that an EMS responder might use?
> - Which categories of responders provide rescue in hazardous areas, and why were they selected for this role?

A specific example of a proactive practice for communication would be employers who promote dialogue with the media. Emergency responders, including EMS responders, can help media representatives before a disaster occurs by providing useful background information to help the media understand how EMS responders work and what conditions put them at undue risk. It is also important for citizens to understand how the risk to the community increases when EMS responders and ambulances must be taken out of commission due to contamination, injury, or illness. Employers might consider training media spokespersons who can help disseminate this message. During an emergency, however, communication with the media must be with one voice through the incident command system (ICS) structure.[7]

The EMS Hazard Assessment

Requirement and Purpose

Employers must conduct hazard assessments to identify the expected hazards associated with EMS

---

[6] Also attempt to answer questions such as, "In this community, where is the line drawn between attempting to save a victim and maintaining the safety and health of the EMT (...and of the second EMT who would attempt to save the first EMT)?" Is that line set at a realistic point? Clearly defined expectations help employers communicate these expectations to employees, who may require supportive training. It is counterintuitive for a medic (regardless how unqualified) to stand back and NOT respond to a victim in need of rescue. In a hazardous substance incident, however, the danger may be increased if unqualified individuals respond unsafely. EMS responders must be trained and equipped to safely perform their duties in the environments they will encounter.

[7] The Hospital Incident Command System (HICS), an ICS for hospital/healthcare organizations is described in Appendix I.

OSHA®
Occupational Safety and
Health Administration

responders' roles in responses to reasonably anticipated worst-case scenarios in the community. These hazard assessments are required, for example, by OSHA's Personal Protective Equipment standard (1910.132(d)(2)) and give the employer the information needed to select PPE (i.e., eye, hand, foot, head protection) that is suitable for the EMS responders' work conditions. The employer must produce a written certification that the hazard assessment has been conducted (see page 27 for further discussion of the necessary documentation).

EMS responders must also consider anticipated airborne hazards when selecting respiratory protection for EMS responders. Factors to consider include identifying the substance, making a reasonable estimate of exposure levels, and predicting the contaminant's chemical state and physical form. When it is not possible to identify the contaminant or estimate worker exposure levels, the employer must consider the atmosphere to be immediately dangerous to life and health (IDLH). (29 CFR 1910.134(d)(1)(iii)). As discussed in the section, Summary of OSHA's Recommendations for Training and PPE, both PPE and respiratory protection are prescribed for IDLH environments by the HAZWOPER standard, which requires an SCBA respirator and Level A or Level B PPE, as defined by Appendix B of the HAZWOPER standard.

Not all EMS responders must be equipped to work in an IDLH environment. In particular, EMS responders may wear lower levels of respiratory protection and PPE in areas where the Incident Commander has determined that an IDLH environment does not exist. In that case, EMS responders must wear respiratory protection and PPE at least as protective as that which the Incident Commander has determined necessary to protect them from the hazards that exist in the area. Frequently, the PPE and respiratory protection permitted at these times is less cumbersome, more comfortable, and less costly than that required for work in IDLH environments.

It is for the purpose of identifying protective equipment suitable for these reduced hazard situations that the employer must perform the most detailed hazard assessments and respiratory hazard evaluations. The information they gather will help employers who wish to equip their EMS responders in this manner with the information needed to choose respiratory protection and PPE that will provide reasonable protection under the range of non-IDLH conditions workers are most likely to encounter in their assigned roles. Fortunately, although the employer is ultimately responsible for ensuring that its EMS responders are adequately

protected, much of the information needed to select the protective equipment is available from other sources within the community.

Sources of Hazard Assessment Information in the Community

Numerous resources are available to employers of EMS responders regarding hazards for which the community expects to prepare. In seeking hazard assessment information, employers should place emphasis on obtaining information most relevant to EMS responders. One particularly good place to start, which does not require original research, is with a local hospital's Hazard Vulnerability Analysis (HVA).[8] Drawing on the hazard assessment findings of other organizations and experts will save time and speed the process of determining what training and PPE are necessary, as well as aiding in the creation of the employers' ERP.

LEPCs are community planning organizations that most likely have as members employers of EMS responders and other experts involved in emergency management.[9] There is no requirement for a community to form an LEPC, but there are a number of benefits including access to low or no-cost training and other preparedness activities. One of the requirements LEPCs must fulfill is to conduct a community hazard assessment. The *Hazardous Materials Emergency Planning Guide*, published by the National Response Team and available at: www.nrt.org, provides guidance on how to perform these assessments. This process may help employers prepare their own hazard assessment if necessary. Where mutual aid agreements increase the possibility of EMS personnel responding to other

---

[8] The Joint Commission on Accreditation of Hospital Organizations (JCAHO) requires that accredited hospitals develop and review an HVA. In a 2004 survey, 84 percent of 575 hospitals reported having completed a collaborative threat and vulnerability analysis of the community (Barbara et al., 2006). When asked, "Do you perceive your hospital to be at increased risk for any of the following hazards or threats (check all that apply)," 76 percent of the 575 respondents listed "hazardous materials" as a perceived risk at their hospital, while 47 percent listed "terrorism" and 26 percent listed "nuclear concerns." For comparison, risks associated with severe weather (e.g., floods, tornados, and winter storms) were mentioned by 42 percent, 62 percent, and 67 percent of the hospitals, respectively. Describing a weakness of the study, the authors reported that slightly more than half of the hospitals that responded to the survey were located in urban areas and 35 percent were trauma centers. Small, rural, and unaccredited hospitals were less likely to have responded and so they were underrepresented in the survey results. A lack of historic experience with certain types of events (e.g., terrorism) also limits the strength of this subjective information.

[9] Visit http://yosemite.epa.gov/oswer/lepcdb.nsf/Home Page?openForm to see listings for LEPCs by location.

communities, employers should also consider the hazards which those other communities perceive as increased risks.

Information provided by community members can be used to concentrate or supplement areas of concern suggested by public information sources, such as the Hazardous Substances Emergency Events Surveillance (HSEES) system database.[10] Review of these data suggest the types of substance release incidents most likely to result in exposures and casualties (Hall et al., 1994; Hall et al., 1995; Hall et al., 1996; Berkowitz et al., 2004; Kaye et al., 2005). Appendix E contains a summary of these analyses. When reviewing the HSEES information, however, employers should note that some of the HSEES data analyses and similar sources predate the September 11, 2001 attack on the World Trade Center and do not include consideration of terrorism.

Other sources of information on community hazards include:

- Local HAZMAT teams.

- EPA's Envirofacts (www.epa.gov/enviro/index_ java.html).

- The spill reports database of the National Response Center (available through www.nrt.org or at www.nrc.uscg.mil/index.html).

- Community right-to-know information available from the LEPC or the State Emergency Response Commission.

- National Fire Incident Reporting System available from the U.S. Fire Administration at www.usfa.dhs.gov/fireservice/nfirs.

Other local organizations can also provide information gathered from their activities. Examples of these resources include the local or state fire marshal, local health authorities, and county agriculture agents. On a national scale, the Homeland Security Council and U.S. Department of Homeland Security have published a list of 15 scenarios, considered "the worst-case" situations for which the nation needs to prepare. Hazardous substance release is among them (Homeland Security Council, 2005). While these scenarios may be too broad for individ-

ual employers to use in planning to protect EMS responders, the employers may find these scenarios referenced in community plans.

Include EMS Responder Health and Safety Experience in Hazard Assessments

OSHA permits the use of industry and company experience in the hazard assessment. Appendix O – Occupational Health Hazard Experience of EMS Responders – contains information on the published experiences of EMS responders, both during hazardous substance release events and during routine responses. When conducting hazard assessments for EMS responders, employers may draw upon this information, then supplement it with information related to anticipated local conditions. These employers may also incorporate information on their own health and safety experience (e.g., from occupational injury and illness records or other employer records).

Incorporating EMS Responder Preparation into an Effective Emergency Response Plan

Emergency response plans describe policies and procedures developed by employers, based on the roles EMS responders will serve and the hazard assessments associated with these roles in the community. An OSHA compliance instruction notes that if employers have chosen to have their own workers respond to releases that would require an emergency response, the employers must develop emergency response capabilities that are appropriate to their individual situations (OSHA, 2007-CPL-02-02-073). Employers' ERPs must describe the steps that the employers have taken to prepare all of their workers (in this case EMS responders) who would be expected to respond in the event of a hazardous substance release.

Employers must have an ERP that explains what steps are being taken to be sure that all of their EMS responders:
- Are adequately trained for their intended job duties.
- Are properly equipped for the intended tasks.
- Are capable of responding in a safe manner.
- Are managed by competent leaders.

(OSHA CPL-02-02-073, 2007)

In evaluating ERPs, OSHA looks for signs of an effective program, including (but not limited to):

---

[10] Also in 1989, the Agency for Toxic Substances and Disease Registry (ATSDR) implemented an active state-based hazardous substances emergency events surveillance system (HSEES) in an attempt to adequately characterize the public health consequences of hazardous substance releases. A hazardous substance emergency event is defined as uncontrolled or illegal releases or threatened releases of chemicals or their hazardous by-products. The HSEES database collects information on events, chemicals, victims, injuries and evacuations. Analysis of the HSEES data helps identify risk factors associated with hazardous substances releases.

OSHA®
Occupational Safety and Health Administration

- Pre-emergency planning and coordination, such as integration with a local or state emergency response plan (LERP or SERP).
- Identification of the types of hazardous substance release emergencies that would require response.
- Clearly defined personnel roles.
- Clear lines of communication.
- Worker training that is consistent with their roles.
- Procedures to be followed if personnel or equipment require decontamination.
- Selection of PPE for personnel performing decontamination.
- An inventory of PPE and emergency response equipment, including instructions for use, their limitations, and the circumstances under which they will be used.
- Procedures for critiquing responses (to help improve future responses).

The previous sections suggested methods employers can use to identify their workers' anticipated roles in emergency responses involving hazardous substance releases. The following sections are intended to help employers consider the HAZWOPER training and PPE needs of their EMS responders based on their anticipated roles and responsibilities.

Training

Summary of Existing Training Guidelines for EMS Responders

The U.S. Department of Transportation's (DOT), National Highway Traffic Safety Administration (NHTSA) developed a National Standard Curriculum (NSC) for EMTs at all provider levels. These guidelines constitute the basic national entry-level training requirements for EMS responders, accepted by most states, while leaving the option for state and local authorities to tailor the guidelines to best meet local needs. NHTSA's NSC introduces the topic of hazardous substances and response associated with hazardous substance releases, but does not automatically prepare EMS responders to meet the expected levels of competence required by OSHA's HAZWOPER standard, nor does it provide information relevant to local community emergency response plans (OSHA, 2004-Gantt). To meet the requirement for emergency first responder HAZWOPER training at either the awareness or operations level, the trainer must:

- Augment the NSC with additional hazardous substance response information.

- Tailor the training to the individual worker's assigned duties.

- Augment the operations level training duration to meet minimum HAZWOPER requirements (see Training Duration, below [for First Responder Operations Level]).

Other organizations also offer supplemental training for EMS responders. Examples include the training activities for DOT's Hazardous Materials Emergency Preparedness program, the Federal Emergency Management Agency's (FEMA) Emergency Management Institute course offerings, and the National Institute of Environmental Health Sciences' (NIEHS) Worker Environmental Training Program. These programs also require tailoring to include local community response plans to ensure that EMS responders understand their assigned duties.

Applicability of HAZWOPER Training to EMS Responders

The scope of paragraph (q) of OSHA's HAZWOPER standard (or the parallel state standards in states with OSHA-approved State Plans) covers "emergency response operations for releases of, or sub-stantial threats of releases of, hazardous substances without regard to the location of the hazard." (29 CFR 1910.120(a)(1)(v)). Specifically, paragraph (q) covers employers whose workers are engaged in emergency response no matter where it occurs, unless those workers are engaged in hazardous waste site operations.[11]

HAZWOPER paragraph (q) outlines requirements for advance planning, training, medical monitoring and PPE for emergency responders. Several specific categories of emergency response personnel are defined in this paragraph, including first responder awareness level and first responder operations level. OSHA's compliance directive for paragraph (q) specifically includes "emergency medical services" responding to a hazardous substance release area.

OSHA has clarified that the HAZWOPER standard only applies to emergency releases, or substantial threats of releases, of hazardous substances. "HAZWOPER does not necessarily apply to every incident in which an individual requiring medical treatment is contaminated with [a] hazardous substance. OSHA cannot require HAZWOPER training for incidents outside the scope of the standard, although such training may be beneficial." (OSHA, 1995-Nechis). The scope of the HAZWOPER standard does not cover "incidental releases," releases that are limited in quantity and pose no emergency or significant threat to the safety and health of workers in the immediate vicinity.

An example is a tanker truck receiving a load of HAZMAT at a tanker truck loading station. At the time of the accidental spill, the product can be contained by employees in the imme-

---

[11] The exceptions indicate that paragraph (q) does not apply to activities at uncontrolled hazardous waste sites that are on EPA's National Priority Site List (NPL), cleanup operations at sites covered by the *Resource Conservation and Recovery Act of 1976* (RCRA), voluntary cleanup operations at sites recognized by federal, state, local or other governmental bodies as uncontrolled hazardous waste sites, and operations involving hazardous waste that are conducted at treatment, storage, disposal (TSD) facilities regulated by 40 CFR Parts 264 and 265 pursuant to RCRA; or by agencies under agreement with U.S. EPA to implement RCRA regulations (see paragraphs (a)(1)(i) through (a)(1)(iv) of 29 CFR 1910.120). The standard goes on to state that only paragraph (q) of the standard applies to emergency response activities unless the response involves an identified hazardous waste site (29 CFR 1910.120(a)(2)(iv)). Other provisions of the HAZWOPER standard do not apply to emergency response operations except where paragraph (q) specifically refers to the other provisions.

diate vicinity and cleaned up utilizing absorbent without posing a threat to the safety and health of employees. Thus, this situation is considered an incidental release, not an emergency release covered by HAZWOPER (OSHA, 2007-CPL-02-02-073).

The principles of risk assessment, PPE, decontamination and training apply equally.

As further clarification, OSHA explains in Appendix A of the HAZWOPER compliance directive that personnel responding to an overturned aircraft leaking jet fuel would likely be performing emergency response due to the significant and uncontrolled hazards posed by the aircraft and jet fuel. These personnel would be conducting operations such as fire fighting, passenger rescue and working to stop the release of jet fuel. However, a fuel spill from a tanker truck that can be absorbed, neutralized or otherwise controlled by employees in the immediate release area through the placement of absorbent pads may qualify as an incidental release, providing that there are no significant health or safety hazards (OSHA, 2007-CPL-02-02-073).[12]

Regarding acts of terrorism and natural disasters, an OSHA directive on the HAZWOPER standard explains that, while employers are not required to prepare specifically for terrorist events (which are considered unforeseeable workplace emergencies),[13] employers must prepare for emergencies that release hazardous substances, regardless of the cause of the release.

The release of chemicals or hazardous substances into a workplace, whether caused by an accidental release or by a terrorist event would...be considered a hazardous substance (HAZMAT) incident. All emergency responders and employees performing emergency response efforts for such releases would, therefore, fall under 1910.120(q). The level of emergency responder training must be based on the duties and functions to be performed by each responder.

Workplaces located in areas prone to natural phenomena, such as earthquakes, floods, tornadoes, and hurricanes, and potentially subject to a 'substantial threat of release of hazardous substances' are covered by 1910.120. The ERP required in 1910.120(q)(1) must include responses to emergencies caused by such natural phenomena. The requirement of the ERP clearly states in paragraph (q)(1), that emergency response plans 'shall be developed and implemented to handle anticipated emergencies prior to the commencement of emergency response operations.' This means that employers in areas prone to natural phenomena should anticipate whether such natural phenomena are likely to cause releases of hazardous substances and, if so, to incorporate emergency response procedures to such natural phenomenon in their ERP (OSHA CPL 02-02-073, 2007).

Medical personnel, including EMS responders, are *not typically* first on the scene, but because EMS responders do usually respond in the first phase of an incident, they are likely to be involved at the scene of an emergency during the initial risk assessment, rather than having the advantage of a fully characterized hazard assessment when they arrive. Although many scenes initially considered to potentially involve a hazardous substance release can be quickly reclassified, EMS responders sent to the scene of an emergency must be appropriately trained to work in a suspect environment. This means that EMS responders need instruction on how to think beyond the confines of "medical care" so they can work safely and function as part of the incident command system (ICS). At any evolving emergency scene, EMS responders' duties might range from keeping themselves out of situations that present a hazard and are beyond the capacity of their level of training or available protective equipment, to contributing observations and information about the patient's condition that will influence triage decisions and help decision-makers better characterize the hazards at the site.[14] These considerations point to the need for first responder awareness level training as a minimum.

---

[12] Other OSHA standards will still apply, such those as for hazard communication (29 CFR 1910.1200), permissible exposure limits (29 CFR 1910.1000), respiratory protection (29 CFR 1910.134), and personal protective equipment (29 CFR 1910.132).

[13] "OSHA does not consider terrorist events to be foreseeable workplace emergencies for purposes of standards requiring employers to anticipate and prepare for such emergencies." (OSHA, CPL 02-02-073, 2007).

---

[14] For example, patients treated by the EMS responder might exhibit signs and symptoms that suggest the presence or identity (i.e., raise the index of suspicion) of a hazardous substance release.

First on the Scene

The situation of an EMS responder arriving first on the scene could arise more or less frequently depending on the experience and practices in that community.

For example, first responders in some communities may be obliged to stop if they happen upon a transportation accident that has just occurred. The accident might involve a hazardous substance release. Furthermore, some communities dispatch EMS responders, rather than police or firefighters, to certain medical 911 calls, but it is possible that those calls could involve hazardous substances that were not reported during the 911 call.

If, in the initial stages of a response, the EMS responder could temporarily be the decision-maker at the site until a more qualified incident commander arrives, then that EMS responder requires both first responder operations level training [29 CFR 1910.120(q)(6)(ii)] and incident commander training (29 CFR 1910.120(q)(6)(v)).

Some EMS responders should have additional levels of training. Although not normally the case, occasions exist when EMS responders could be the first to arrive on a scene (see above text box, First on the Scene). In this case, the EMS responder could have interim authority as the initial incident commander (IC) for the brief period between incident discovery and the time that a correctly trained IC arrives at the scene. The EMS responders who could find themselves performing this role need additional instruction on how to think beyond the confines of medical care (see above box "First on the Scene"). Furthermore, specific EMS responders might be designated to provide special services, such as rescue, decontamination, or treatment of trapped patients in an area of higher hazard. These individuals also require, at a minimum, first responder operations level training. Online training resources on the National Incident Management System (NIMS) and the Incident Command System (ICS) are available through the Federal Emergency Management Agency (FEMA) Website.[15]

EMS Responder Roles Requiring HAZWOPER Training

First Responder Awareness Level Training

First responder training at the awareness level is the minimum level of training required for EMS responders who respond to emergencies (including 911 calls) and might be first on the scene of an emergency, but would not be expected to treat or handle a contaminated patient (OSHA, 1991-McNamara). These EMS responders would not be designated to serve in any capacity on a decontamination team at the site of the emergency release, nor would they enter an area where contaminants could be present. This group of EMS responders would be responsible for notifying authorities if they encountered suspect hazardous substances at a scene and are expected to stay alert to signs that a release might have occurred, but would not attempt to rescue patients or treat contaminated patients (OSHA, 1991-McNamara). Rather, these EMS responders would wait for other properly trained and equipped first responders to bring thoroughly decontaminated patients to a safe area where the EMS responders could treat them. A higher level of training (HAZWOPER first responder operations level training) is required if an EMS responder could be assigned to rescue, treat, or participate in decontamination of victims of a hazardous substance release, or provide these services under any mutual aid agreement or employer contract with the community. OSHA does not believe that all EMS responders need to be trained to treat contaminated victims (OSHA, 1992-Chapman); however, those who will perform this service must be properly trained to do so. First responder awareness level training should adequately prepare EMS responders to use professional judgment to distinguish between the situations for which the responder is qualified to act and those which require a higher level of training and PPE.

Training Duration, Topics and Competencies

First responder training requirements for the awareness level appear under 29 CFR 1910.120(q)(6)(i). This section does not require a specific minimum training duration, but outlines topics that must be covered (competencies the worker must acquire). In the HAZWOPER compliance directive, OSHA mentions that although the standard does not set a minimum number of hours for this training, "such courses often run from 4 to 12 hours" (OSHA, 2007-CPL-02-02-073). The HAZWOPER standard allows an alternative to the first responder awareness level training requirement. Training can be waived if the worker has had sufficient experience to objectively demonstrate competency in specific areas. The required training topics (or areas of competency) are listed in 29 CFR 1910.120(q)(6)(i), or the parallel State Plan standards, and include:

---

[15] To access NIMS and ICS online training, go to http://www.fema.gov/emergency/nims/nims_training.shtm#0.

OSHA®
Occupational Safety and
Health Administration

- An understanding of what hazardous substances are, and their associated risks during an incident.[16]

- An understanding of the potential outcomes associated with an emergency created when hazardous substances are present.

- The ability to recognize the presence of hazardous substances in an emergency.

- The ability to identify the hazardous substances, if possible.

- An understanding of their role in the employer's emergency response plan, including site security and control and the *DOT Emergency Response Guidebook*.

- The ability to realize the need for additional resources and to make appropriate notifications to the communications center.

Although not required, OSHA recommends as a best practice that training include information on risk assessment and risk management to enable EMS responders to understand and identify the limitations of their expected role.

- Recognizing the types of situations that could include a hazardous substance release.

- Placards, labels, common hazard rating schemes (e.g., National Fire Protection Association [NFPA] hazard warning diamond) and other indicators of hazardous substances.

- Recognizing signs or symptoms of hazardous substance exposure in patients and responders.

- The steps the EMS responder is expected to take if a scene or patient is discovered to be contaminated with a hazardous substance (or substance suspected of being hazardous).

- The extent and limitations of the EMS responder's training and PPE (what they are and are not prepared to do).

Annual Refresher Training

Annual refresher training is required for workers trained at the first responder awareness level. The class content must be adequate to maintain the EMS responder's competence, and the employer must document the training or the method used to demonstrate the EMS responder's competence. Employers may also use actual or drill responses to

---

[16] As noted previously, a hazardous substance is any substance to which exposure may result in adverse effects on health or safety of workers. This includes biological agents, substances listed by U.S. DOT as hazardous materials, and substances classified as hazardous wastes. See Appendix A – Glossary for a more detailed definition.

fulfill the refresher training requirement.

First Responder Operations Level Training

Employers must provide HAZWOPER first responder operations level training to designated EMS responders who are expected to treat patients before they are thoroughly decontaminated. This includes EMS responders who perform decontamination, which could bring the EMS responder into contact with contaminated individuals (OSHA, 1991-McNamara; OSHA, 1992-Levitin). It also includes EMS responders who "enter the danger area to perform rescue or treat contaminated victims." (OSHA, 1995-Nechis).

Training Duration

Training requirements for first responder operations level appear under 29 CFR 1910.120 (q)(6)(ii), which indicates a minimum training duration of 8 hours and outlines topics to be covered (competencies the worker must acquire). Both the required competencies and training time for medical personnel trained at first responder operations level were confirmed in an interpretive letter (OSHA, 2003-Bolt). OSHA, however, allows these topics (but not the minimum training time) to be tailored to better meet the needs of first responders. Training that is relevant to the required competencies counts toward the 8-hour requirement, even if the training is provided as a separate course. For example, training on PPE that will be used during patient decontamination activities may be applied towards the 8-hour minimum first responder operations level training requirement, regardless of whether the PPE training is conducted as part of a specific HAZWOPER training course or as part of another training program (OSHA, 1992-Levitin).

First responder awareness level training completed by a worker also counts towards that individual's 8-hour requirement for first responder training at the operations level. This point is clarified in a letter of interpretation issued by OSHA:

"…if you spend two hours training employees in the required competencies for First Responder Awareness Level as described in 29 CFR 1910.120(q)(6)(i)(A)-(F), then you would need to spend at least six additional hours training employees in the required competencies for First Responder Operations Level as described in 29 CFR 1910.120(q)(6)(ii)(A)-(F). Depending on the employees' job duties and prior education and experience, more than eight hours of training may be needed." (OSHA, 2003-Bolt).

Option to Demonstrate Competence

As with first responder awareness level training, the HAZWOPER standard allows workers to demonstrate competence in specific areas as an alternative to the 8-hour training requirement (29 CFR 1910.120(q)(6)(ii)). OSHA reaffirmed this point in a letter of interpretation (OSHA, 2003-Bolt). However, it is important to recognize that in the typical EMS responder setting, it might be difficult to ensure that workers have sufficient experience to waive all the training requirements. Many EMS responders lack extensive experience with higher levels of respiratory protection along with, as the studies cited in Appendix O demonstrate, performance of decontamination activities.

Topics for Training or Demonstration of Competency

The HAZWOPER standard requires that workers trained at the first responder operations level shall have received at least 8 hours of training or have had sufficient experience to objectively demonstrate competency (e.g., in exercises and drills) in the following areas (1910.120(q)(6)(ii)):

All of the topics previously listed for first responder training at the awareness level, plus the additional topics listed here.

- Knowledge of the basic hazard and risk assessment techniques.

- Knowledge of how to select and use proper PPE. [A critical aspect is knowing both when PPE is useful, and under what circumstances it will NOT provide adequate protection.]

- An understanding of basic hazardous materials terms.

- Knowledge of how to perform basic control, containment, and/or confinement operations within the capabilities of the resources and PPE available.

- Knowledge of how to implement basic decontamination procedures.

- An understanding of the relevant standard operating procedures and termination procedures.

Although not required, OSHA recommends as a best practice that training topics be tailored to reflect EMS responders' anticipated duties and might include details such as:

- Understanding the community emergency operations plan and EMS responders' role in the response, including who will provide decontamination services.

- Recognizing signs and symptom of exposure to hazardous substances that they could encounter at emergency response scenes in jurisdictions they might cover (including those areas covered by mutual aid agreements).

- Assessing site safety, including risks to EMS responders.

- Specific training on hazardous risk assessment during encounters with contaminated patients.

- Selecting and using appropriate PPE. (See paragraphs below titled *Associated Training – PPE* and *Associated Training – Respiratory Protection*.)

- Employing patient decontamination procedures. (See Best Practices for Pre-ambulance Patient Decontamination, below.)

Annual Refresher Training

Annual refresher training at the first responder operations level is required under 1910.120(q)(8)(i), or the parallel State Plan standards; however, the length of the refresher training is not specified. Instead, the standard requires that workers trained at the first responder operations level shall receive annual refresher training of sufficient content and duration to maintain their competencies, or shall demonstrate competency in those areas at least yearly. Employers may also use actual or drill responses to fulfill the refresher training requirement.

Documenting How Training Requirements Are Met: Employers of EMS responders must document that initial and refresher training was performed, or alternatively, keep a record of how the EMS responder demonstrated competence in the required areas. This is particularly important whenever workers are allowed to satisfy any portion of the training requirement through other related training or through demonstration of competence. The HAZWOPER standard requires, and an OSHA letter of interpretation confirms, that the employer must certify in writing the comparable training or demonstrated competencies (OSHA, 2003-Bolt).

Associated Training

The following subsections briefly describe training that employers must provide EMS responders who use PPE and/or respiratory protection. This training can count towards the 8-hour requirement for first responder operations level training.

OSHA®
Occupational Safety and
Health Administration

It is also important that the level of training be compatible with the PPE that is provided to EMS responders. Over-equipping workers may encourage them to attempt activities beyond the level for which they are trained. If workers require a higher level of protection, consider whether a higher level of training, including HAZWOPER training, is also needed.

Associated Training – PPE

The first responder operations level training related to the use of PPE must include topics as required by OSHA's PPE standard (29 CFR 1910.132). Under this standard, training must be provided to each worker who is required to use PPE. At a minimum, that training must cover the following:

- Recognizing when PPE is necessary.

- Identifying what PPE is necessary.

- Demonstrating how to properly put on, remove, adjust, and wear PPE.

- Understanding the limitations and hazards of PPE.

- Understanding the proper care, maintenance, useful life and disposal of PPE.

Workers must demonstrate their understanding of the training by showing that they can use the PPE properly, prior to wearing it in the workplace. Refresher training is required when the worker cannot demonstrate proficiency in the proper care and use of the PPE, when changes in the workplace render the previous training inadequate, or when changes in the type of PPE to be used render the previous training inadequate. The employer must maintain a written record of worker PPE training. It is the employer's responsibility to assess the full range of the EMS responder's expected duties and provide PPE and PPE training accordingly. This assessment must include the worker's expected role during reasonably anticipated worst-case scenarios.

Associated Training – Respiratory Protection

First responder training at the operations level also must include training required by OSHA's Respiratory Protection standard (29 CFR 1910.134), or the parallel State Plan standards. Specifically, any worker who must wear a respirator must be trained in the proper use and limitations of that device prior to its use in the workplace. The training must be comprehensive enough that the worker is able to demonstrate knowledge of the seven training topics specified in the standard and outlined below. The worker also must be able to demonstrate compe-

tence in wearing the complete PPE ensemble, including respirator, protective garment, gloves, boots, and any other safety equipment required for the worker's role. Refresher training is required at least annually, or sooner if changes in the workplace or type of respirator render previous training inadequate. Refresher training is also required if the worker does not demonstrate proficiency in the proper care and use of the respirator, or at any other time when retraining appears necessary to ensure safe respirator use.

At a minimum, training under OSHA's Respiratory Protection standard must cover the following topic areas:

- The nature of the respiratory hazard, and why a respirator is needed.

- Respirator capabilities, limitations and consequences if the respirator is not used correctly.

- How to handle respirator malfunctions and other emergencies.

- How to inspect, put on, remove, use and check seals on the respirator.

- How to maintain the respirator face/face seal integrity (e.g., through proper grooming, cleaning, and correct use).

- Maintenance and storage procedures.

- When to change cartridges on air purifying respirators (APRs).

- Additional prescribed procedures relating to SCBAs (if used), such as monthly inspections and ensuring breathing air quality.

- How to recognize medical signs and symptoms that may limit or prevent effective use of a respirator.

- General requirements of the respiratory protection program.

Sources of Training and Curricula

Several examples of HAZWOPER first responder operations level training curricula are available for employers preparing EMS responders to conduct decontamination activities. Examples include the *Hazardous Materials and Terrorist Incident Prevention Curriculum Guidelines* (HMEP, 1996). However, these curricula are not necessarily designed as 8-hour presentations. Many curricula are longer, while others are shorter and intended for use when workers are able to demonstrate competence in specific areas. See Appendix H for an additional discussion on options for first responder training at the awareness and operations levels for EMS personnel.

If employees who only provide inter-facility transport are unexpectedly called on to aid a contaminated victim, those individuals may be considered skilled support personnel and receive special on-the-spot training.

However, if repeatedly called upon to treat accident victims contaminated from HAZWOPER incidents, the EMS employer must train and designate the employees to the First Responder Operations Level (OSHA, Nechis, 1995).

(See the related discussion of skilled support personnel, below).

First responder training is offered at both the awareness and operations levels through a number of public and private organizations. An increasing number of hospitals offer (or coordinate) local classes tailored to medical personnel.[17]

EMS Responder Roles that Require No HAZWOPER Training

As noted previously, if an employer has not agreed to be designated in a state or local emergency response plan to respond to a hazardous substance release, then the employer may not have any obligation to train workers under the HAZWOPER standard (OSHA, 1995-Nechis). For example, employers are not obliged to provide HAZWOPER training to an EMS responder whose work involves only patient transport between medical treatment facilities, as long as no agreements exist that could increase the EMS responder's involvement in emergency response including hazardous substances.

It also bears repeating that employers may not designate an EMS responder as exempt from HAZWOPER training if it is anticipated that the EMS responder could suddenly be activated to provide 911 response. This prohibition holds even for "strictly medical" 911 calls – since some of these calls can involve unanticipated hazardous substance release (e.g., scenes that upon arrival are discovered to involve a methamphetamine laboratory). Similarly, an EMS responder cannot be exempt from HAZWOPER training if the employer has entered into a mutual aid agreement that could result in the EMS responder responding to an emergency or a 911 call, or if the employer has signed support contracts or made arrangements with the community, local organizations, or neighboring communities that

could result in the EMS responder being sent to the site of an emergency.

Because a worker without HAZWOPER training might not be equipped to identify the presence of a hazardous condition and make the decision to stay away, an untrained EMS responder who happens upon the scene of an emergency should not approach the site.

Skilled Support Personnel

The HAZWOPER standard allows for the case where a worker is not expected to serve in an emergency response capacity, but nevertheless is suddenly called upon (e.g., as a one-time occurrence) to provide emergency care at a scene involving hazardous substance release. When this occurs, the worker is termed *skilled support personnel*. An EMS responder who has been exempt from HAZWOPER training by the employer (such as those discussed above), but is unexpectedly called on to aid a contaminated patient, or perform other work at the scene of a hazardous substance release, is considered skilled support personnel. Other examples of skilled support personnel include a medical specialist or a trade person, such as an electrician. These individuals must receive expedient orientation to site operations, immediately prior to providing such services (OSHA, 1997-Whittaker). An EMS responder without HAZWOPER training might treat and transport patients that have been "…totally and thoroughly decontaminated and removed from the danger zone. However, in this case, while working as skilled support personnel, these EMS responders should be given an initial briefing at the site…" prior to providing this service (OSHA, 1991-McNamara). This briefing would also be needed for EMS responders trained at the first responder awareness level, who are suddenly called upon to provide decontamination services, which would require first responder training at the operations level. The briefing for skilled support personnel is intended to provide the individual with information necessary to safely do a specific job at a specific incident site and typically assumes no prior HAZWOPER training.

The following quotation from an OSHA letter of interpretation emphasizes this important point:

"…if an EMS [squad] is not designated in any emergency response plan, but finds that they are repeatedly called upon to treat accident victims contaminated from a HAZWOPER incident, these workers cannot be considered skilled support personnel and the EMS employer must train and designate the workers to the First Responder Operations Level." (OSHA, 1995-Nechis).

---

[17] Additional resources to assist with the development of training can be found at: www.osha.gov/SLTC/emergencypreparedness/index.html.

When an EMS responder is unexpectedly called upon to respond to a hazardous substance incident as skilled support personnel, the EMS responder must receive an orientation that provides information on:

- Nature of the hazard (if known).
- Expected duties.
- Appropriate use of PPE.
- Other appropriate safety and health precautions (e.g., decontamination procedures).

If a respirator will be needed, these personnel also must be medically cleared for respirator use before the respirator is worn. An acceptable fit test and proper grooming to ensure a good face/facepiece seal is required if the responder will wear a **tight-fitting** respirator. These steps are required by 29 CFR 1910.134 (Respiratory Protection), or the parallel State Plan standards.

While a just-in-time briefing during the response is the only required training for these personnel, time and resource limitations inherent in a crisis likely will diminish the effectiveness of such training. **This is another reason why employers of EMS responders should diligently consider the broad range of conditions under which their workers might be called to serve and provide an appropriate level of HAZWOPER training.**

> An employer cannot allow workers to be designated as skilled support personnel as an alternative to providing appropriate, initial, and refresher HAZWOPER training.

Relevance of Other HAZWOPER Training Levels to EMS Responders

An OSHA letter of interpretation discusses the roles of EMS responders and other emergency responders at the scene of a hazardous substance release. "Standard emergency medical practice dictates that EMS personnel are to survey the accident scene and remain away from the hazard area until it is safe to approach. In the case of a HAZWOPER roadway emergency, the incident needs to be brought under control by more highly skilled emergency responders before it would be permissible for EMS personnel, including those certified at the first responder operations level, to enter to perform rescue or provide medical treatment." (OSHA, 1995-Nechis).

First responder training beyond the operations level is not necessary for worker activities that are restricted to medical treatment and decontamination. However, many EMS responders have qualifications at higher levels of HAZWOPER training. These are EMS personnel who elect to be cross-trained to serve an expanded role (e.g., firefighter, HAZMAT team member), and might receive other levels of HAZWOPER training as needed in support of those additional roles. For example, firefighters commonly obtain additional education to qualify as EMS responders (in addition to continuing to qualify as firefighters) and some EMS personnel are trained at the Hazardous Materials Technician or Hazardous Materials Specialist level to serve on special HAZMAT teams. Any HAZWOPER training that an EMS responder receives beyond the first responder operations level would be to support the role of firefighter or HAZMAT team member. The EMS responder might, in the capacity of firefighter, enter dangerous areas to perform non-medical activities such as controlling a hazardous substance release or performing rescue, for which the higher level of HAZWOPER training is required.

Conclusions Regarding EMS Training

Employers must use the information at their disposal to make informed decisions regarding suitable levels of HAZWOPER training for their EMS personnel. Although there may be some EMS personnel for whom HAZWOPER training is not necessary, OSHA believes that after a critical review of community expectations and community threats, most employers will find that at a minimum first responder awareness level training is appropriate for all their EMS responders and that some of these personnel also require first responder operations level training. In some communities, contract language referring to HAZWOPER initial and refresher training will promote EMS personnel qualifications in this regard.

Personal Protective Equipment

The best practices presented in this document indicate the minimum PPE that OSHA generally anticipates will be needed to protect EMS responders under various conditions. However, as with any generalized protection, OSHA's PPE selection for EMS personnel offers more protection against some hazards than others. If an employer or incident commander determines that EMS responders could reasonably anticipate encountering a specific known hazard, the employer or incident commander also must determine whether this generalized protection must be supplemented to more fully protect against the specific hazard.

In order to complete the hazard assessment and PPE selection process, each employer must consider the role the EMS responders will play in the communities in which they might be called upon to operate. Employers should also consider additional information available from community sources regarding the range of hazards that EMS responders could encounter during reasonably anticipated worst-case scenarios (OSHA, 2002-Hayden). When these sources point to a specific substance or situation from which the employer should protect EMS responders, the employer must confirm that PPE selection provides effective protection against that hazard. In rare situations, the employer may find it necessary to augment the PPE specified in this document for unknown hazards in order to help ensure protection against specific known hazards (e.g., by tailoring glove selection to address an identified, specific hazard, or by stocking additional supplies).

Employers must adopt a more specialized level of protection (such as atmosphere-supplying respirators [ASR]) when the EMS responder's role in the community or hazard assessment indicates that a higher level of protection is necessary, such as when EMS responders could be subjected to an environment immediately dangerous to life and health (IDLH).

PPE selection will vary based on the working conditions of EMS personnel. OSHA suggests that employers of EMS personnel provide workers with the minimum PPE that will offer protection against a reasonably anticipated worst-case scenario, including catastrophic or terrorist incidents. It is important to note, however, that the minimum PPE for the reasonably anticipated worst-case scenario may differ between locales. For example, after evaluating (1) the roles that these responders could be called upon to fill in the community and (2) the reasonably anticipated hazards that EMS responders could encounter in their community, an EMS employer should review these best practices and select the minimum PPE that would protect against the most serious credible situations.

> "If only one level or type of PPE will be available, it is appropriate for that PPE to cover the worst-case situation. EMS agencies might also wish to provide other types of PPE for less-than worst-case situations (e.g., the hazard is identified and risk is reduced). If an adequate level of PPE is not carried on the ambulance, the agency needs to have a provision for getting it to the site where it is needed." (OSHA Stakeholder Comments, 2006)

For most employers of EMS responders, the reasonably anticipated worst-case scenario is likely to involve the release of *unidentified or uncharacterized* hazardous substances with potential for secondary contamination. In many areas, the worst case could include the possibility that the unidentified substance would be a *CBRNE substance*. Where community expectations restrict the EMS responders to treating patients only after the hazardous substance is characterized, or to treating only patients who have been thoroughly decontaminated by other EMS personnel (e.g., properly equipped HAZMAT team members), then the most serious exposure scenario might only involve characterized or identified hazardous substances, or possibly limited quantities of partially characterized hazardous substances. OSHA, however, believes that in most communities, certain EMS responders cannot be assured of such a limited role during a widespread mass casualty incident. As a result, PPE selection for EMS responders in these communities should be based on the need to provide decontamination at the scene of the incident and the need to offer emergency medical services before the hazardous substance has been characterized. The number of EMS responders who should be trained and equipped

with PPE allowing them to provide decontamination services will depend on the community's expectations and Hazard Vulnerability Analysis.

Employers should keep in mind that once a hazardous substance is identified or characterized, the PPE can be adjusted to appropriate levels, as determined by the incident commander. Employers should be prepared to provide adjusted PPE suitable for the most common anticipated situations in the community.

Required Written Documentation for Respirator and PPE Selection Process

Employers selecting respiratory protection and PPE must consider factors outlined in OSHA's Respiratory Protection standard (29 CFR 1910.134) and Personal Protective Equipment standard (29 CFR 1910.132). For both respirators and PPE, a primary selection factor is the hazards that workers are likely to encounter and both standards contain requirements for written documentation (see text box - Written Documentation of Hazard Assessment for PPE Selection). Several other selection factors are listed in the following subsections and details on all factors are provided in the respective OSHA standards.

Written Documentation of Hazard Assessment for PPE Selection

Under 1910 Subpart I, the employer must perform a hazard assessment to select appropriate personal protective equipment for the hazards that are present, or likely to be present, including foreseeable emergencies. The hazard assessment must be in the form of a written certification as described in 29 CFR 1910.132(d)(2).

The employer shall verify that the required workplace hazard assessment has been performed through a written certification that identifies the workplace evaluated; the person certifying that the evaluation has been performed; and the date(s) of the hazard assessment. The written certification must also clearly identify the document as the certification of hazard assessment.

The hazard assessment provision applies only to 29 CFR 1910.133 (eye and face protection), 1910.135 (head protection), 1910.136 (foot protection), and 1910.138 (hand protection). Although it does not apply to 29 CFR 1910.134 (respiratory protection) and 1910.137 (electrical protective devices), the

Respiratory Protection standard does contain specific requirements for evaluating respiratory hazards. The employer must include procedures for selecting respirators in the written respiratory protection program as described in 29 CFR 1910.134. As part of the selection process:

The employer shall identify and evaluate the respiratory hazard(s) in the workplace; this evaluation shall include a reasonable estimate of employee exposures to respiratory hazard(s) and an identification of the contaminant's chemical state and physical form. Where the employer cannot identify or reasonably estimate the employee exposure, the employer shall consider the atmosphere to be IDLH. (29 CFR 1910.134(d)(1)(iii))

Assessing the Need for Respiratory Protection

Respiratory Protection Required for EMS Responders

Respiratory protection requirements are well defined for specific emergency response situations. OSHA's HAZWOPER standard and letters of interpretation dictate the levels of protection that OSHA requires for EMS responders in cases of high hazard and when the hazard is very low. The respiratory hazard evaluation that employers conduct helps them define the types of respiratory protection that incident commanders are most likely to designate at scenes once the hazard is adequately characterized. Employers of EMS responders who could be called upon to play a role in emergency response must equip their workers to work safely in their assigned roles (OSHA, CPL 02-02-073, 2007).

Types of Respiratory Protection Available

Appendix J provides an overview of respiratory protection types, facepieces, and their associated advantages and disadvantages. Employers of EMS responders should consult Appendix J while considering the respiratory protection that their workers would need to perform specific emergency response roles. Practical matters, such as how to ensure that the correct respiratory protection is available at the scene, need to be considered as part of the emergency response plan. OSHA believes that EMS responders will not be able to work safely if they are designated to fill roles for which the required PPE will not necessarily be on hand.

National Institute for Occupational Safety and Health (NIOSH) Approval and Chemical, Biological, Radiological, Nuclear (CBRN) Certifications

Respiratory protection for EMS responders must always be of a type approved by NIOSH. Additionally, in any location where CBRN substances are a threat, the respirator should also be NIOSH-rated for use in CBRN environments. In addition, CBRN respirators offer advantages of having passed additional testing to assure ruggedness and structural durability.

Respiratory Protection for an Identified or Characterized Hazard

The incident commander is responsible for determining an appropriate level of respiratory protection for EMS responders at emergency scenes involving the release of a known hazardous substance(s), or entry into the dangerous area of the scene after the substance is characterized. However, in some circumstances, OSHA's HAZWOPER standard prescribes the level of protection. Specifically, an SCBA respirator is required when an IDLH atmosphere is present, including occasions when the hazardous substance is unidentified or information is inadequate to rule out an IDLH environment. OSHA's Respiratory Protection standard requires that for an IDLH environment the SCBA must be configured as a full facepiece pressure demand SCBA certified by NIOSH for a minimum service life of thirty minutes, or as a combination full facepiece pressure demand supplied-air respirator (SAR) with auxiliary self-contained air supply (29 CFR 1910.134 (d)(2)(i)(A) and (B)). Furthermore, Appendix B of the HAZWOPER standard indicates that where an IDLH environment is present, Level A or Level B PPE are required, depending on whether the hazard includes a substance that can be absorbed or is hazardous to the skin (requiring Level A) or not (Level B permitted). For a description of these PPE levels, see Appendix N – General Description and Discussion of the Levels of Protection and Protective Gear.

Other Requirements Related to Respiratory Protection

If EMS responders will need to wear respiratory protection, OSHA requires that the employer develop a respiratory protection program that explains how the employer meets the requirements outlined in OSHA's Respiratory Protection standard (29 CFR 1910.134). The program must cover topics such as the procedures used for selecting respirators; how

medical evaluations and fit testing are provided; methods for ensuring that respirators are properly used, cleaned and maintained; worker training; and how the program's effectiveness is evaluated.

Gloves, Boots and Garments

As is the case with respiratory protection, the actual conditions will dictate the level and type of PPE required to protect an EMS responder. Some considerations for gloves, boots and protective clothing are presented in the following sections. Regardless of the selection, the provisions of the Bloodborne Pathogens standard (29 CFR 1910.1030) would apply. As previously discussed, the employer must certify that a hazard assessment has been performed as part of the PPE selection process.

Gloves and Boots

No single glove or boot material will protect against every substance. Base the selection on the type and extent of anticipated contact with hazardous substances. Consider the type of substances, the effect of dermal exposure, patient symptoms, and the likely interventions that contaminated patients might require, then select protective gear that best allows critical patient treatments while fully protecting the EMS provider.

Most glove manufacturers offer detailed guides to glove materials and their chemical resistance. Butyl rubber gloves generally provide better protection than nitrile gloves for chemical warfare agents and most toxic industrial chemicals that are more likely to be involved in a terrorist incident, although the converse applies to some industrial chemicals. Foil-based gloves are highly resistant to a wide variety of hazardous substances and could also be considered when determining an appropriate protective ensemble. Employers of EMS responders must select materials that cover the specific substances that the employer has determined that EMS responders reasonably might encounter. However, given the broad scope of potential contaminants, OSHA considers it important for employers to select materials that protect against a wide range of substances. A double layer of gloves, made of two different materials, or foil-based gloves will resist the broadest range of chemicals.

A combination of gloves, for example, butyl gloves worn over inner nitrile gloves, is often the best option for use by EMS responders during emergencies and mass casualties involving hazardous substances. However, responders are advised to select the combination that best meets

their specific needs. Between gloves that offer adequate worker protection, select the model(s) that minimize impact on delivering the types of patient interventions that are most likely to be needed.

Glove thickness is measured in mils, with a higher number of mils indicating a thicker glove (1 mil equals 1/1000 of an inch). Using common examples, exam gloves are often approximately 4 mil, while general-purpose household (kitchen) gloves are 12–16 mil, and heavy industrial gloves might be 20 to 30 mil.

Depending on the dexterity needed by the EMS responder, the glove selection can be modified to allow for the use of a glove combination that is thinner than that usually recommended for the best protection. As an example, the U.S. Army Center for Health Promotion and Preventive Medicine (USACHPPM) recommends that medical personnel working with patients potentially contaminated with chemical warfare agents or toxic industrial chemicals wear a combination of chemical protective gloves, such as butyl rubber gloves over inner nitrile gloves (USACHPPM, 2003a). Because thicker gloves offer greater protection, USACHPPM recommends a butyl glove with a minimum thickness of 14 mil (over a 4 or 5 mil nitrile glove). However, with increased thickness comes greater loss of manual dexterity and hand fatigue. When advanced medical procedures must be performed before decontamination, thicker gloves might be too awkward, and, therefore, it might be necessary to use a butyl rubber glove of 7 mil over the nitrile glove, or a 14 mil butyl rubber glove alone (USACHPPM, 2003a).

> When manual dexterity is required, a 14 mil butyl glove, or a 7 mil butyl glove over a 4 to 5 mil nitrile glove, may be the best options; however, these gloves should be changed frequently to minimize the chance of exposure if gloves tear, abrade, or are chemically degraded. (OSHA Stakeholder Comments, 2006).

Hendler et al. (2000), as cited in USACHPPM (2003a), conducted a study to determine the effect of full PPE (including 12-mil "tactile" gloves and a full facepiece mask) on intubation performance. Clinicians wearing this equipment could perform endotracheal intubation effectively (i.e., the tube was inserted in sufficient time), but the procedure did take longer than it would have without PPE. Intubation delays would cause subsequent decontamination procedures and medical treatment to be delayed by a corresponding amount of time. Some

incidents may have injured patients in such a way that routine emergency care cannot be rendered until the patient is decontaminated to assure adequate protection to the medical team.

If sterility is required and decontamination is not possible before performing medical procedures, a double layer of disposable 4 to 5 mil nitrile gloves might be the best option (USACHPPM, 2003a). Not all sources recommend double gloves; for example, the U.S. Army Soldier and Biological Chemical Command's (SBCCOM) [now called the Research, Development and Engineering Command, or RDECOM] Domestic Preparedness Program (DPP) recommends butyl rubber gloves for personnel performing decontamination operations and casualty care (SBCCOM, 2000). Among the sterile gloves readily available, those made of nitrile offer the best resistance to the widest range of substances. Thinner gloves fail (deteriorate, tear, rip) more rapidly than thicker gloves and, therefore, if they must be used, these gloves should be inspected and changed more frequently. Thinner gloves should be changed when contaminated or as soon as feasible if they are torn, punctured, or when their ability to function as a barrier is compromised.[18]

In general, the same material selected for gloves will also be appropriate for boots. Because boot walls tend to be thicker than gloves, boots of any material are likely to be more protective than gloves of the same material. Military vinyl overshoes (designed to be worn over combat boots) are now commercially available at competitive costs and have been approved by the military for protection against chemical warfare agents.

Protective Garments

The optimal garment material for EMS responders will vary depending on the responder's role and should be a subject of the employer's hazard assessment. Except for particularly harsh climates, standard uniforms may be sufficient for EMS responders in the cold zone. As discussed below, the selection is more complex for responders who could find themselves in the warm zone. See Appendix K for links to additional information on

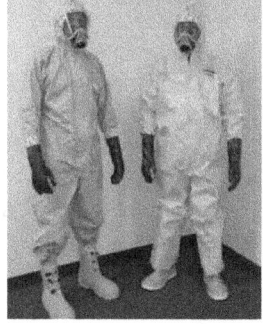

Photo courtesy of Frank Califano

---

[18] For additional information on recommended glove materials and chemical breakthrough of specific substances, see the NIOSH *Recommendations for Chemical Protective Clothing: A Companion to the NIOSH Pocket Guide to Chemical Hazards.* Available at www.cdc.gov/niosh/ncpc/ncpc2.html

thermal stress and working in cold and hot conditions, including working in chemical protective suits.

In the warm zone, EMS responders will need garments that protect against a wide range of chemicals in liquid, solid, or vapor form (phase). Because EMS responders might become contaminated with liquid or solid (dust) contaminants through physical contact with a contaminated patient, the ideal fabric will repel chemicals. Additionally, the optimal garment will restrict the passage of vapors, both through the suit fabric and through openings in the suit. Finally, optimal clothing is also sufficiently flexible, durable, and lightweight for long-term wear (up to several hours) during physically active work.

A variety of broad-spectrum protective fabrics and designs may be appropriate, depending on the situations and hazards that the employer anticipates EMS responders reasonably might be expected to encounter. Several commercially available products include: Tyvek® F, Tychem® CPF3, Tychem® CPF4, Tychem® BR, Tychem® LV, Tychem® SL, Zytron® 100, Zytron® 200, Zytron® 300, Zytron® 400, Zytron® 500, and Zytron® 600, ProVent® 10,000, and DuraVent® 2.8. Note, however, that OSHA does not test, endorse, or recommend specific products. Before selecting products or materials, contact the manufacturer for specific application guidance.

Fabric and suit manufacturers can provide laboratory testing information regarding specific materials.[19] For example, Tyvek® F has been tested extensively by military organizations and accredited testing laboratories. As another example, the SBCCOM (now called RDECOM) DPP tested vapor-blocking properties of six different protective suits in a simulated, high-vapor environment. In the results tabulated below, the Tyvek® F suit (ProTech model) offered a protection factor of 42 (vapor levels outside the suit were 42 times higher than inside the suit), which was approximately twice the protection than was provided by the next best performing suits. Traditional Tyvek® (protection factor of 4) was twice as protective as a standard police uniform (protection factor of 2). These suits were tested by placing sensors for the test vapor under the suits at 17 specific body locations. Volunteers wore the protective gear while performing the activities normally

associated with an actual first responder chemical response (but did not involve physical acts, such as patient handling or handling needles and injections, that would likely be required of EMS responders) (SBCCOM, 2003). Results are summarized in Table 1.

Table 1.

Results of Simulation Tests on Several Chemical Suits

Suit Configuration	# Suits Tested	Protection Factor
Standard [Police] Uniform	2	2
Tyvek® Protective Wear Suit	4	4
Tychem® 9400 Protective Suit	4	17
Kappler® Tychem CPF4 Protective Suit	4	18
Tychem® SL Protective Suit	5	24
Tyvek® ProTech F Protective Suit	5	42
Source: SBCCOM, 2003.		

The ability of protective garment fabric to withstand physical abrasion and tearing is also important. If their role could involve assisting non-ambulatory contaminated patients or victims trapped in the hot zone, EMS responders might subject the protective garments to physical stresses that should be considered in garment selection. The NFPA Standard No. 1994 on Protective Ensemble for First Responders to CBRN Terrorism Incidents offers criteria for evaluating the performance of protective garments, including detailed specifications for bursting, puncture and tear resistance, as well as garment seam specifications (NFPA, 2007).

Additionally, the Interagency Board has begun publishing a list of standard products, including PPE, for use in national emergencies (IAB, 2007).

As a rule of thumb, if the employer has determined that an EMS responder's role in a response could involve using SCBA, the responder should also be outfitted with broad spectrum chemical protective clothing. However, chemical protective clothing is generally semi- or impermeable. Anytime an EMS responder wears semi-permeable or impermeable clothing, the risk of heat stress increases substantially. See Appendix K for a discussion of thermal stress on EMS responders working in hot and cold environments.

Modifying PPE Selections Based on Available Information

Flexibility in prescribing respiratory protection and PPE is particularly important. Employers of EMS responders must be prepared to provide their work-

---

[19] Some chemical-protective fabric manufacturers provide Web-based services for comparing their products. For example, chemical permeation and recommended usage charts for DuPont's Tychem® line and related fabric types appear at www2.dupont.com/NOWApp/DPPRequestGateway/0/pct/?command=ACProductComparisonHome and Kappler's Zytron fabrics are compared at www.kappler.com/techdata_main.html.

ers with respiratory protection and PPE that is at least as effective as that which the incident commander might dictate for the situations EMS responders could reasonably be expected to encounter in their designated roles. The employer's ERP should include information on the PPE that the employer will make available to workers. Because this guide recommends Levels A and B for most situations involving EMS responders, such protection provides adequate eye protection. Therefore, additional discussion on eye protection is not warranted.

Proper Size and Fit of PPE

The size and fit of PPE is as important as selecting appropriate materials and configurations. Poorly fitting respirators, gloves, footwear, or protective clothing offer a reduced level of protection. Specifically, ill-fitting equipment might gape, leak, fall off, cause tripping, or create other serious safety hazards. Employers must consider fit in the selection of protective gear for EMS responders, as required by OSHA's General Requirements for personal protective equipment (29 CFR 1910.132(d)(1)(iii)). EMS responders who wear tight-fitting respirators must be fit tested before the first time they wear the respirator in the field and again each year. See Respiratory Protection for an Identified or Characterized Chemical Hazard, above, for a summary of additional requirements associated with respiratory protection.

Considerations for Effectively Using, Maintaining and Storing PPE

Once PPE decisions have been made, the employer should obtain PPE in adequate quantities and sizes to meet the needs of those EMS responders who will wear the equipment. Consider protective gear compatibility when making purchases, so that one piece of equipment does not interfere with the functioning of another. PPE used to prevent hazardous material exposure (e.g., a respirator) must be compatible with other 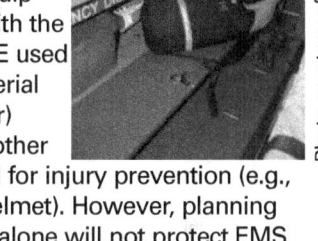 safety equipment required for injury prevention (e.g., protective eyewear or a helmet). However, planning and purchasing decisions alone will not protect EMS responders.

Many types of PPE, such as respiratory protection (excluding filtering facepieces) require ongoing inspection, maintenance, worker training, medical monitoring, and recordkeeping. For additional information on this topic, consult OSHA's standard on

Respiratory Protection (29 CFR 1910.134) and OSHA's *Small Entity Compliance Guide for Respiratory Protection* at www.osha.gov/Publications/sec grevcurrent.pdf.

> EMS responders who are asked to perform activities or work in areas for which they are not equipped should bring this to the attention of the IC (or designated safety officer).

In accordance with OSHA's PPE standards, and as discussed in the Training section of this guide, workers must be trained to use PPE effectively and to recognize when PPE will not provide adequate protection. EMS providers risk injury if they become exposed to dangerous substances due to a false sense of security when using incorrect PPE, or when wearing PPE improperly (Hick, 2007).

Community expectations for EMS providers' activities and the areas in which they will work must take into consideration each employer's decision about workers' roles, how PPE is distributed, where equipment is stored, and how the employer determines the manner in which personnel are trained to react. Experience has shown that when proper PPE is not readily available, EMS responders are reluctant to pull back and wait for better equipped providers to arrive. Instead, EMS personnel tend to provide medical rescue and care without appropriate PPE, thus exposing themselves to a higher risk (rather than compromising patient care, they compromise their own safety) (Hick, 2007). Personnel training must be adequate to ensure that EMS providers fully understand their limitations (and those of their training and equipment). If EMS providers might encounter contaminated patients seeking medical assistance, provide medical care in a contaminated area or to contaminated patients, or be called upon to support fire department decontamination efforts, these individuals must be trained and equipped to do these jobs safely.

Conclusions Regarding Personal Protective Equipment

Carefully considered EMS responder PPE goes hand-in-hand with the responder's training; only with proper training will EMS responders be able to identify hazardous substance release conditions and understand the limits within which they can work safely with their available PPE. Determining training and PPE needs in advance through a hazard assessment will permit employers of EMS responders to ensure that their workers are prepared for the incidents in which they are expected to participate. The PPE offered to EMS responders should correspond to both the type of training they are provided and to

Photo courtesy of Frank Califano

Summary of OSHA's Recommendations for Training and PPE

OSHA's recommendations are based on the roles that EMS responders could be assigned during emergencies involving hazardous substance releases. OSHA's recommendations on minimum training and PPE for EMS responders assisting patients at hazardous substance release sites generally follow regulatory requirements contained in paragraph (q) of OSHA's Hazardous Waste Operations and Emergency Response (HAZWOPER) standard (29 CFR 1910.120) and associated interpretive letters. In some instances, OSHA also recommends that employers consider offering instruction to certain EMS respon-ders who would not otherwise receive any HAZWOPER training under regulatory requirements, but who OSHA believes might find themselves in a situation where this training would allow them to make better decisions to protect both themselves and other EMS personnel.

Table 2 summarizes OSHA's recommendations and requirements. In the table, the required training and PPE are presented in a matrix, with additional recommendations indicated as relevant. To use the table, locate a typical EMS responder role along the top of the table and a specific hazardous substance response scenario down the left-hand side. Employers may locate the appropriate training and PPE in the cell at the intersection of the designated EMS responder role column and selected scenario row. Figure 1, which follows Table 2, offers simple instructions for using the table.

Table 2. Training, Respiratory Protection, and PPE for EMS Responders

ZONE▸ (EMS Responder Assigned Role) ▸ ▾ Scenario	HOT ZONE (Rescue/Life support) [A] [G]	WARM ZONE (Decontamination/ treatment in warm zone)	COLD ZONE (Treat uncontaminated/ decontaminated patients in clean area)	EMERGENCY TRANS-PORT FOR 911 CALLS (Transport nominally clean or cleaned patients)[K]	INTER-FACILITY TRANSPORT ONLY (Never respond to 911 calls. No mutual aid agreements for emergency response)
CBRNE agent or substance generating IDLH environment at the site[B]	When a skin hazard is present... **Training:** Operations level[C] **Respirator:** SCBA[E] **PPE:** Level A[D] — No skin hazard... **Training:** Operations level[C] **Respirator:** SCBA[E] **PPE:** Level B[D]	When a skin hazard is present... **Training:** Operations level[C] **Respirator:** SCBA[E] **PPE:** Level A[D] — No skin hazard... **Training:** Operations level[C] **Respirator:** SCBA[E] **PPE:** Level B[D]	**Training:** Awareness level strongly recommended[K] (Operations level recommended).[L] **Respirator & PPE:** Only as needed for preventing infection.	**Training:** Awareness level strongly recommended[K] (Operations level recommended).[L] **Respirator & PPE:** Only as needed for preventing infection.	Not applicable
Unknown substance - could be a serious hazard [H]	**Training:** Operations level[C] **Respirator:** SCBA[E] **PPE:** Level A[D,F]	**Training:** Operations level[C] **Respirator:** SCBA[E] **PPE:** Level A[D]	**Training:** Awareness level strongly recommended[K] (Operations level recommended).[L] **Respirator & PPE:** Only as needed to prevent infection.	**Training:** Awareness level strongly recommended[K] (Operations level recommended).[L] **Respirator & PPE:** Only as needed to prevent infection.	Not applicable
Partially character-ized hazard, avail-able information suggests low or moderate hazard	**Training:** Operations level[C] **Respirator:** SCBA, or as indicated by IC based on site charac-terization.[E] **PPE:** Level B, or as indicated by Incident Commander[F] based on site characteriza-tion.[I]	**Training:** Operations level[C] **Respirator & PPE:** As per Incident Commander[E, F I, J]	**Training:** Awareness level strongly recommended[K] (Operations level recommended).[L] **Respirator & PPE:** Only as needed to prevent infection.	**Training:** HazCom[M] (Operations level recommended).[L] **Respirator & PPE:** Only as needed to prevent infection.	Not applicable
Known substance, low or moderate hazard	**Training:** Operations level[C] **Respirator & PPE:** As per Incident Commander (IC)[E] [F, J]	**Training:** Operations level[C] **Respirator & PPE:** As per Incident Commander (IC)[E] [F I, J]	**Training:** Awareness level strongly recommended[K] (Operations level recommended).[L] **Respirator & PPE:** Only as needed to prevent infection.	**Training:** HazCom[M] (Operations level recommended).[L] **Respirator & PPE:** Only as needed to prevent infection.	Not applicable
No emergency response	Not applicable	Not applicable	Not applicable	Not applicable	Routine HazCom train-ing.[M] PPE only as needed to prevent infection.

TABLE ENDNOTES:

[A] This table addresses EMS entry into contaminated areas only to provide medical assistance to patient(s). Entry for other purposes (e.g., controlling the release of a hazardous substance or rescue operations) requires an additional level of competency and implies cross-training with another specialty, such as firefighter or hazardous materials technician. Individuals performing activities other than (or in addition to) patient medical care are covered by other requirements beyond the scope of this document.

[B] IDLH Definition: Immediately dangerous to life or health (IDLH): An atmosphere that poses an immediate threat to life, would cause irreversible adverse health effects, or would impair an individual's ability to escape from a dangerous atmosphere. *OSHA Definition*

[C] Operations level is appropriate for: (1) EMS responders who must enter the danger zone to provide medical assistance (OSHA, 1995-Nechis); (2) EMS responders expected to treat contaminated patients at the release area but at a safe distance from the point of release (OSHA, 2007-CPL-02-02-073).

[D] Select Level A when: (1) The hazardous substance has been identified and requires the highest level of protection for skin, eyes, and the respiratory system based on either the measured (or potential for) high concentration of atmospheric vapors, gases, or particulates; or the site operations and work functions involve a high potential for splash, immersion, or exposure to unexpected vapors, gases, or particulates of materials that are harmful to the skin or capable of being absorbed through the skin; (2) Substances with a high degree of hazard to the skin are known or suspected to be present, and skin contact is possible; or (3) Operations must be conducted in confined, poorly ventilated areas, and the absence of conditions requiring Level A have not yet been determined (29 CFR 1910.120 Appendix B, Part B.I). Select Level B when the type and atmospheric concentration of substances have been identified and require a high level of respiratory protection, but less skin protection (29 CFR 1910.120 Appendix B, Part B.II.) www.osha.gov

[E] Workers engaged in emergency response and exposed to hazardous substances presenting an inhalation hazard or potential inhalation hazard shall wear positive pressure self-contained breathing apparatus while engaged in emergency response, until such time that the individual in charge of the ICS determines through the use of air monitoring that a decreased level of respiratory protection will not result in hazardous exposures to workers. In a chemical, biological, radiological, and nuclear (CBRN) environment, use only a respirator approved by NIOSH for use in a CBRN environment. (1910.120(q)(3)(iv)) www.cdc.gov/niosh/npptl/topics/respirators/cbrnapproved/scba/default.html

[F] Based on the hazardous substances and/or conditions present, the individual in charge of the ICS shall implement appropriate emergency operations, and assure that the PPE worn is appropriate for the hazards to be encountered. (1910.120(q)(3)(iii))

[G] "Standard emergency medical practice dictates that EMS personnel are to survey the accident scene and remain away from the hazard area until it is safe to approach. ...the incident needs to be brought under control by more highly skilled emergency responders before it would be permissible for EMS personnel, including those certified at the Operations Level, to enter to perform rescue or provide medical treatment." (OSHA, 1995-Nechis).

[H] SIGNS OF A CHEMICAL, BIOLOGICAL, RADIOLOGICAL, AND NUCLEAR (CBRN) OR HIGHLY TOXIC AGENT: suspicious circumstances, results from early detection equipment do not rule out CBRN, patients exhibiting symptoms. SIGNS OF AN ONGOING RELEASE: Saturated clothing in an enclosed environment, visible spray/dust in air, flowing substance on surfaces, sound of possible substance release (e.g., gas or spray), visible pooling, explosion at chemical plant – not yet controlled; patients exhibiting symptoms of continuing exposure, unresponsive victims – cause uncertain.

[I] Information to Help Make the Decision that Respirator and PPE Level Can Be Reduced: Rationale for reducing respiratory protection levels should include one or more of the following: (1) Air monitoring/screening tools to confirm potential inhalation hazard is of a level for which a decreased level of respiratory protection will not result in hazardous exposures to employees (sensors, meters, direct reading instruments, swab and wipe sample readers, dip indicators [pH paper], battery operated detectors) indicates that the chemical class is not one that is highly toxic or is one of low volatility, that bioagent is not of significant concern, that ionizing radiation activity is not present in area, or that a secondary CBRN agent is not present in area. (2) Clear evidence that the hazardous substance is not highly toxic or volatile (e.g., credible placard or label on leaking containers or tank). (3) Statement about contents from person in control of the source of the release. (4) Visible evidence strongly suggests agent of lower toxicity (e.g., leaking from fuel tank of vehicle with a diesel engine/fuel tank strongly suggests a diesel release; NFPA, Hazardous Materials Information System (HMIS), or equivalent hazard rating scheme label on source container or tank indicates low toxicity). In all cases, flammability and reactivity may also produce hazards that should be taken into consideration when restricting access, or selecting equipment that could be brought into the area, but minimal impact on PPE and training decision in areas where EMS responders would typically work. For the purposes of this document, OSHA understands that other more highly skilled responders would work in areas with high risk of flammability or reactivity.

[J] See Appendix I for summary information on respiratory protection. Consider NIOSH Respirator Selection Logic (2004) (www.cdc.gov/niosh/docs/2005-100) for guidance on choosing minimal acceptable respirator for the reasonably anticipated worst-case scenario.

[K] EMS personnel are often first on the scene and, therefore, should be given first responder awareness level training as a minimum, even if they are not expected to handle contaminated patients. Furthermore, individuals trained at least to the awareness level would identify poorly or incompletely cleaned patients (when decontamination is done by others) (OSHA, 1991-McNamara).

[L] Some stakeholders providing input to this document recommend, and OSHA agrees, that as a best practice any employer that offers emergency response services should be prepared to decontaminate patients, even if the community would normally assign that duty to a fire department or HAZMAT team. In particular, they believe EMS responders may be called upon to decontaminate injured or ill patients, but not necessarily ambulatory uninjured people who might be assisted in decontamination by other emergency responders (OSHA, 2006-EMS Stakeholder Comments).

[M] The Hazard Communication standard (29 CFR 1910.1200) requires training of any workers who may potentially be exposed to hazardous chemicals during their duties. This training can incorporate an overview of the community's ERP to help clarify that this group of workers lacks any role in it (OSHA, 2007-CPL-02-02-073).

Additional Note: See Appendix N for a general description and discussion of the levels of protection and protective gear (e.g., Level A and Level B).

Figure 1. How to Use Table 2

Step 1. Read across the top rows to find the anticipated zone where the EMS responder could work and the responder's role.

Step 3. Then find the EMS responder's Training and PPE needs at the point where the selected Zone/Role column intersects with the selected Scenario row.

Step 2. Read down the left side of the table to find the anticipated worst-case hazardous substance release scenario under which the EMS responder could work.

Step 4. Look up special notes and the reference using end notes that appear after the table.

ZONE► (EMS Responder Assigned Role) ► ▼ Scenario	HOT ZONE (Rescue/Life support) [A] [G]	WARM ZONE (Decontamination/ treatment in warm zone)	COLD ZONE (Treat uncontaminated/ decontaminated patients in clean area)	EMERGENCY TRANS- PORT FOR 911 CALLS (Transport nominally clean or cleaned patients)[K]	INTER-FACILITY TRANSPORT ONLY (Never respond to 911 calls. No mutual aid agreements for emer- gency response)
CBRNE agent or substance generat- ing IDLH environ- ment at the site[B]	**When a skin hazard is present…** **Training:** Operations level[C] **Respirator:** SCBA[E] **PPE:** Level A[D]	**When a skin hazard is present…** **Training:** Operations level[C] **Respirator:** SCBA[E] **PPE:** Level A[D]	**Training:** Awareness level strongly recom- mended[K] (Operations level recommended).[L] **Respirator & PPE:** Only as needed for preventing infection.	**Training:** Awareness level strongly recom- mended[K] (Operations level recommended).[L] **Respirator & PPE:** Only as needed for preventing infection.	Not applicable
	No skin hazard… **Training:** Operations level[C] **Respirator:** SCBA[E] **PPE:** Level B[D]	**No skin hazard…** **Training:** Operations level[C] **Respirator:** SCBA[E] **PPE:** Level B[D]	**Training:** Awareness Level[K] (Operations Level recommended).[C,L] **Respirator & PPE:** Only as needed for preventing infection.		
Unknown substance - could be a serious hazard [H]	**Training:** Operations level[C] **Respirator:** SCBA[E] **PPE:** Level A[D,F]	**Training:** Operations level[C] **Respirator:** SCBA[E] **PPE:** Level A[D]		**Training:** Awareness level strongly recom- mended[K] (operations level recommended).[L] **Respirator & PPE:** Only as needed to prevent infection.	
Partially character- ized hazard, avail- able information suggests low or moderate hazard	**Training:** Operations level[C] **Respirator:** SCBA, or as indicated by IC based on site charac- terization.[E] **PPE:** Level B, or as indicated by Incident Commander[F] based on site characteriza- tion.[I]	**Training:** Operations level[C] **Respirator & PPE:** As per Incident Commander[E, F I, J]	**Training:** Awareness level strongly recom- mended[K] (operations level recommended).[L] **Respirator & PPE:** Only as needed to prevent infection.	**Training:** HazCom[M] (operations level rec- ommended).[L] **Respirator & PPE:** Only as needed to prevent infection.	Not applicable
Known substance, low or moderate hazard	**Training:** Operations level[C] **Respirator & PPE:** As per Incident Commander (IC)[E] [F, J]	**Training:** Operations level[C] **Respirator & PPE:** As per Incident Commander (IC)[E] [F I, J]	**Training:** Awareness level strongly recom- mended[K] (operations level recommended).[L] **Respirator & PPE:** Only as needed to prevent infection.	**Training:** HazCom[M] (operations level rec- ommended).[L] **Respirator & PPE:** Only as needed to prevent infection.	Not applicable
No emergency response	Not applicable	Not applicable	Not applicable	Not applicable	Routine HazCom train- ing.[M] PPE only as needed to prevent infection.

OSHA®
Occupational Safety and Health Administration

Best Practices for Pre-Transport Patient Decontamination

Patient decontamination is critical to patient safety, to the protection of EMS personnel, and to continuing EMS operations. Many communities place responsibility for decontamination activities on the fire department or incident response personnel, without directly involving EMS responders. Other communities ask EMS responders to assist with the process. Some stakeholders providing input to this document recommended that any employer that offers emergency response services should be prepared to decontaminate patients, even if the community would normally assign that duty to a fire department or HAZMAT team. In particular, they believe EMS responders may be called upon to decontaminate injured or ill patients, but not necessarily ambulatory uninjured people who might be assisted in decontamination by other emergency responders (OSHA, 2006-EMS Stakeholder Comments).[20]

Regardless of which responders will perform decontamination, OSHA believes that EMS responders who might be sent to the scene of a release will be better prepared to recognize an inadequately decontaminated patient if they understand the basic decontamination process, even if these EMS responders are not expected to be involved in patient decontamination.

As a best practice, OSHA recommends that employers provide information on decontamination practices to all EMS responders who could be assigned a role in a hazardous substance response. Additional detailed training on performing decontamination is required for EMS responders whom the employer has designated to perform decontamination.

Current accepted decontamination practices focus on removing the patient's clothing, cleansing with soap and water, then rinsing. When these steps are followed carefully, patient exposure is significantly decreased and patients pose less risk to EMS personnel, transport vehicles and equipment.

Removing Contaminated Clothing and Personal Effects

Studies estimate that removing contaminated clothing can reduce the quantity of contaminant associated with victims by an estimated 75 to 90 percent (Macintyre et al., 2000; Vogt, 2002; USACHPPM, 2003a).[21] Modeling studies that help quantify exposures during decontamination and patient handling activities suggest that victims' clothing can hold a significant amount of contaminant. Removing contaminated clothing as soon as possible will reduce both patient and responder exposure levels (Schultz et al., 1995; Georgopoulos et al., 2004). The sooner contaminated clothing and effects are removed the less these potential sources will contribute to exposure levels.

Clothing and personal items that are contaminated should be sealed in double plastic bags to eliminate them as a source of continuing exposure.

Many community plans provide for some patient privacy and protection from harsh weather during decontamination. The plans also often call for the provision of tags to label bagged personal belongings with the owners' names. These provisions can help improve patients' compliance with decontamination procedures.

Cleansing with Soap and Water

Decontamination with soap and water remains the best practice for most contaminants under most circumstances of mass decontamination. Initial rinsing can often be started quickly and will help physically remove water-soluble and particulate contaminants, while a soap that dissolves grease will help remove other substances.

Hurst (1997) notes that "the most important and most effective decontamination after any chemical or biological exposure is that decontamination done within the first minute or two after exposure" and that "after years of research world wide, simple principles that consistently produce good results are still recommended." Specifically, timely physical removal of the contaminating substance is critical. However, "which decontamination method is used is not as important as how and when it is used." (Hurst, 1997).

OSHA realizes that, although generally considered a beneficial practice, 5 minutes of flushing with

---

[20] The stakeholders feel, however, that it makes less sense to suggest that EMS responders decontaminate ambulatory uninjured people (OSHA EMS Stakeholder Comments, 2006).

[21] The percentage of contaminant reduction depends on the type of clothing the victim was wearing when exposed. The estimates may be somewhat lower (down to 50 percent) for victims wearing short pants or skirts and higher (up to 94 percent) for victims exposed to biological warfare agents while wearing protective military uniforms (USACHPPM, 2003a).

rinse water may not always be practical in the field. It serves primarily as a benchmark to guide decision making. USACHPPM recommends 1-minute rinsing from head to toe with tepid water (slightly warm, not hot) after removal of contaminated clothing, followed by a more thorough decontamination by washing with a soap with good surfactant properties (e.g., a liquid soap such as hand dishwashing detergent), tepid water and soft sponges. Avoid stiff brushes and vigorous scrubbing, which can damage the skin and increase the chance that the contaminant would be absorbed by the patient's skin. USACHPPM recommends these procedures for most classes of contaminants, except reactive metal dusts, for which a soft dry brush should be used to remove most of the material from the skin. (USACHPPM, 2003a).

Assistance for Non-Ambulatory and Ambulatory Patients

Non-ambulatory patients can require a substantial proportion of the decontamination team's time and effort. EMS responders designated as decontamination team members are likely to experience the greatest exposures while assisting these patients.[22] The team members should take steps to identify possible sources of contamination and limit their exposure to those sources, as well as the exposure of patients and any EMS responders who may assist the patients later. For example, it is possible to use specific procedures for removing patients' clothing to minimize both decontamination team and patient exposures. One such procedure is to use blunt-nose scissors to cut away clothing, rather than pulling it off. Practical exercises have shown that seatbelt cutters also work well for removing clothing and further reduce the chance of accidental injury.[23] In contrast, tugging on clothing can produce a wringing action that might distribute contaminant on the patient, decontamination team members, and the surrounding area (in addition to unnecessarily shifting a patient who may have spinal injuries). As noted previously, once removed, the clothing should be immediately placed into a sealed container.

Some communities may ask ambulatory patients to assist by performing some of the decontamination steps themselves. Specifically, minimal-

ly exposed patients who are able can help by removing their own clothing and personal effects. They may even begin wetting and cleansing themselves, although these and subsequent steps should be supervised (if not performed) by a responder trained in decontamination procedures. When ambulatory patients assist with these initial decontamination steps during large-scale incidents, decontamination of all patients may be more expedient, and the risks to responders (e.g., from handling contaminated clothing) are reduced.

The methods decontamination team members use to decontaminate themselves and remove (doff) PPE also impact their own exposure. ATSDR (2001) and Appendix M offer examples of procedures used by some teams.

EMS responders might find the following review of basic decontamination steps helpful:

1) Activate the emergency decontamination plan.

2) Learn as much as possible (as soon as possible) about the location of patients, the contaminant, its hazards, and associated symptoms. Previous arrangements with other first responder agencies can improve how information flows to responders.

3) Arrange for decontamination equipment to be delivered to a suitable location. Some systems are heavy and cumbersome – in addition to the need for an adequate area of relatively level ground, consider factors such as vehicular access to deliver equipment and also eventually to provide ambulance service to patients who require it.

4) Activate the decontamination system and assemble the decontamination team. These individuals should be pre-designated by the community plan so that they will be properly trained and have drilled with the available equipment prior to the emergency. Also in advance, the community should consider the need for staffing multiple decontamination lines (for responders, ambulatory patients, and non-ambulatory patients; or males and females), which can increase patient compliance and/or process efficiency. Consider by whom and where decontamination for critically ill/injured patients will be performed.

5) Perform any medical monitoring (e.g., vital signs) of decontamination team members, if specified by the community or EMS agency plan.

6) Put on PPE.

---

[22] OSHA understands that decontamination teams will consist of firefighters, HAZMAT team members, and/or EMS personnel who are FULLY qualified to do so and are wearing adequate protective equipment.

[23] Seatbelt cutters are not as useful for cutting through thick tape around responder's boots; shears work better for this type of material.

7) Triage patients to determine which individuals require decontamination and provide critical medical treatment to stabilize them before decontamination.

8) Direct or assist patients (ambulatory and non-ambulatory) in removing contaminated clothing and securing personal property as soon as possible (within minutes of arrival).

9) Place clothing and other contaminated items in a plastic bag that can be sealed (or when available, place items in an approved hazardous waste container and cover). Ensure that waste bags/containers are isolated and remain outdoors so that the items are not a continuing source of exposure.

10) Perform gross decontamination with water (extensive amounts, if available), such as from a hose. More time-consuming technical decontamination may be necessary to completely remove contaminant. This more thorough decontamination procedure involves washing patients using soap, with good surface-active properties (i.e., soaps that help oil dissolve in water), and water (preferably tepid water to improve patient compliance). Pay particular attention to the back and hair on the head or body. Make sure that hair wash water falls away from the body, if possible. Remove all obvious contamination on a patient with gentle blotting or brushing, never rub or irritate the skin. Avoid abrasive materials (such as "gritty" soaps). This step should also include copious rinsing, especially when dealing with acids or bases. [See discussion, below.] Ambulatory patients may be able to clean themselves under direction of the decontamination team.

11) Inspect patients to evaluate the effectiveness of decontamination. Guide decontaminated patients to the medical treatment area (away from any possible contamination). Return inadequately decontaminated patients to the shower area and repeat cleansing.

12) Decontaminate equipment and the decontamination system (if not disposable).

13) Decontamination team removes PPE and decontaminates themselves. The order in which PPE is removed during responder decontamination can help minimize additional exposure. See Appendix M for an example of a sequence for putting on (donning), decontaminating, and removing (doffing) PPE.

14) Patient inspection provides a final check to ensure that contaminant is not carried into clean areas.

Decontamination procedures, like PPE use, can be modified once the contaminant is identified; decontamination team members who are cleansing patients to remove known contaminants can tailor procedures as appropriate. For example, a longer rinse might be beneficial for contamination in the eyes, or for contamination involving corrosive, sticky, or oil-soluble substances. Organizations such as the Centers for Disease Control and Prevention (CDC) and the U.S. Department of Homeland Security offer specific recommendations for decontaminating patients exposed to individual hazards, such as ionizing radiation (CDC, 2003; U.S. Department of Homeland Security, 2003).[24]

Determining the adequacy of decontamination efforts is a recurring issue in community preparedness discussions. If it was known that patients were exposed to nerve agents and a decontamination team had access to appropriate testing media (e.g., surface testing tapes), this confirmation could be helpful. Although contaminant detection equipment is available for certain other hazardous substances (such as radiological hazards), in most cases confirmation that a patient has been carefully washed by a trained decontamination team still offers the best assurance of safety for EMS responders, vehicles and equipment. As previously discussed, OSHA strongly recommends that employers train to the first responder awareness level all EMS responders who could transport decontaminated patients from a hazardous substance emergency site, and as a best practice train them as first responders at the operations level.

Decontamination in Low Water Situations

Decontamination with extensive amounts of water remains the preferred method; however, for low water situations, other methods can help physically remove contaminant from patients. Several military and civilian organizations are investigating decontamination aids for use in situations when little or no water is available or when cold weather makes water less practical. These methods include targeted application of available water, bulk absorbents and reactive foams.

Once contaminated clothing is removed, spot decontamination can be performed using little water targeted to the skin that was originally exposed (typically the hands and head/hair). Using this method, it might be possible to perform gross

---

[24] The International Commission on Radiological Protection (ICRP) and the National Council on Radiation Protection and Measurements (NCRP) also offer guidance for radiological incidents.

decontamination with a hand-pump sprayer and a few gallons of water.

Hurst (1997) reviewed decades of literature on decontamination methods and noted that an application of flour, followed by wet tissue wipes offers some benefit in reducing the amount of chemical substances left on the skin. Nevertheless, bulk dry absorbents tend to be most useful (and have traditionally been used) for decontaminating large surface areas and points where contaminant has pooled. The best absorbent for a job depends on the contaminant, but any non-reactive substance with a large porous surface area has potential to serve as a sorbent. Materials considered by the U.S. Army for use in cold weather would also serve under conditions where little water is available; suggested practices for conducting gross decontamination include blotting patients with sorbent substances such as paper towels, flour, sand, dirt, an oil absorbent, or diatomaceous earth (Fuller's earth) with the intent of removing harmful material from the patient as quickly as possible (SBCCOM, 2002). As noted previously, patients' clothing should be removed as soon as possible to achieve the maximum benefit.

Gross decontamination with sorbent should be followed up as soon as feasible with a warm water wash. Various foams and creams may play a role in the future, but at this time these products are not approved for use on human skin (see Appendix L - Decontamination Foam and Barrier Cream).

Vehicle and Equipment Decontamination

Prevention is the best policy for protecting vehicles from contamination. Some industrial chemicals can be neutralized, but many will be difficult to remove from porous materials and cracks/ crevices in the interior. If contaminated, the vehicle may need to be taken out of service.

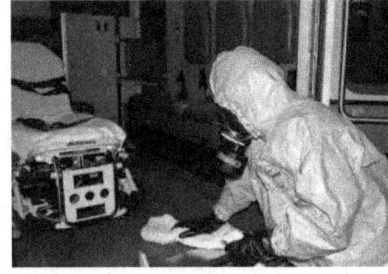

Photo courtesy of Frank Califano

Decontamination of non-porous equipment materials follows a similar process to decontamination of skin (wash with extensive amounts of water and soap, rinse thoroughly, inspect carefully), although equipment can be scrubbed. Porous materials are more difficult to clean effectively and most likely will need to be discarded with other waste from the response and decontamination effort. An OSHA letter of interpretation advises eliminating or

minimizing soft plush surfaces where they might need to be decontaminated later (OSHA, 1994-Bays).

Discovering that a Patient in the Ambulance is Contaminated

EMS providers should make every effort to prevent ambulances from becoming contaminated. Contamination of an ambulance, and the EMS personnel associated with it, could cause them to be removed from service and decrease the availability of these critical resources. Representatives of the EMS community requested guidance in addressing this possible scenario.

OSHA believes that prevention is the first line of defense for preserving emergency medical resources. EMS responders should communicate with other first responders and decontamination teams regarding the extent of patient exposure and the decontamination processes used to clean patients. This information will help ambulance operators ensure that only uncontaminated/clean patients are loaded into the vehicle. EMS responders who suspect residual contamination on a patient should not hesitate to suggest that the patient be returned to the wash area for additional cleaning.

In practice, however, it is possible that EMS personnel could discover evidence of contamination associated with a patient who is already being transported, although that patient was believed to be clean.[25] In this situation, efforts should focus on minimizing further spread of the contaminant and on (further) decontamination. Ambulance operators should take the following steps:

En Route

- Notify the receiving hospital that the incoming patient shows evidence of possible contamination so that decontamination procedures can be activated.

- Verify that all clothing and personal effects are completely removed and sealed in plastic bags (double layer).

- Take available steps to contain the spread of contamination to vehicle and personnel (e.g., wrap patient in disposable tarp or blanket if allowed by patient care protocol).

---

[25] It is also possible that EMS responders might be instructed to transport a contaminated patient. In this case, the responders should confirm that the incident commander is aware that such an action may cause the ambulance and crew to be taken out of service.

OSHA
Occupational Safety and
Health Administration

- Alert the incident site that a patient in transit shows signs of contamination (describe the evidence) so that ongoing patient handling and decontamination procedures at the site can be modified appropriately.

Upon Arrival at the Receiving Hospital

- Treat EMS responders as victims, requiring decontamination and/or treatment, until it is possible to confirm that they have not suffered ill effects.

- Remove the ambulance from service and arrange to have it surveyed immediately to determine whether it can be placed back in service.

Certain ambulance designs can help reduce exposure to airborne contaminants, but do not prevent exposure. For example, NIOSH investigators researching tuberculosis (TB) exposure controls evaluated the effectiveness of supplemental high efficiency particulate air (HEPA) filtration systems in ambulances (NIOSH, 1996).[26] In tests conducted under similar conditions, airborne particles were cleared more rapidly from the air inside an ambulance equipped with supplemental HEPA filtration than from an ambulance without HEPA filtration. Furthermore, testing showed that "particle clearance could be improved with the use of the rear vent fan" (turned to the "high" setting) in combination with fresh air provided through the ambulance's main heating and cooling system. Running the rear vent fan provided some particle clearance even in an ambulance that was not fitted with HEPA filters, in part because running the vent fan increased air exchange in the ambulance. With the main heating and cooling system, HEPA filtration system, and rear vent all running, the volume of air in the rear compartment of the ambulance was replaced at a rate of almost once per minute (56 air changes per hour). The investigators note that "while supplemental engineering controls such as [HEPA filtration] can improve particulate clearance in the ambulance, they will not eliminate the potential for exposure...." When HEPA filtration systems are used, consult the manufacturer to determine the optimal testing and maintenance schedule (NIOSH, 1996).

Detection Equipment

Detection Instruments

Numerous instruments allow EMS responders to detect contaminant levels with varying degrees of precision. Easy-to-use ionizing radiation meters perform well during emergency medical responses and may be used to evaluate both contaminated patients/equipment and the effectiveness of decontamination processes. EMS responders face a greater challenge in identifying chemically or biologically contaminated individuals at the scene, both before and after decontamination procedures.

The first indication of the need to activate the decontamination team might come from first responders who identify contaminated individuals through an initial interview, by visual observation, by the presence of indicative odors, and through signs that a substance appears to be affecting health. After a patient has been through the decontamination system, to confirm cleanliness, EMS responders currently rely primarily on visual inspection and the extent to which the patient followed prescribed showering procedures. Ionizing radiation detectors effectively contribute valuable screening information. In contrast, for most chemical substances the currently available simple, portable chemical detection equipment can supplement these methods, but do not replace them.

Ionizing Radiation Meters

Ionizing radiation occurs in three major forms – alpha, beta, and gamma radiation.[27] Most radiological substances emit one or more of these forms of radiation. Of the three, alpha radiation, in general, has the highest energy and is most hazardous if ingested or inhaled, but presents minimal hazard outside the body. Beta radiation (typically with less energy) can cause skin burns at close range (i.e., skin contamination). Patients can become contaminated with alpha- or beta-emitting radioactive materials if these materials are released during a hazardous substance incident. Inhalation and ingestion of these particles can be greatly reduced by removing contaminated clothing and washing thoroughly (EPA RERT, 2007).

Two different exposure scenarios are possible for photon/gamma radiation, which exists in the form of energy that passes through the body, causing damage to organs and tissues in its path. The source of gamma radiation could be either (1) gamma-emitting radioactive materials (contaminants released during a hazardous substance incident), or (2) a discrete gamma-emitting source of radiation. In the first case, decontamination procedures will help remove the gamma-emitting materials from skin, which will reduce the radiation exposure, and subsequently the risk, to patients and

---

[26] HEPA filters are capable of removing 99.97 percent of the particles that are less than 0.3 microns in diameter (the most penetrating – or worst case – size).

[27] Photon radiation types include gamma radiation, x-radiation, and "bremsstrahlung" (a type of electromagnetic energy).

responders. In the second case, if only photon/gamma radiation is released from a specific discrete source and no gamma-emitting material contaminants (e.g., dusts) are involved, then gamma radiation will be emitted through the area exposing patients (and responders) in the area until the source is removed from the area or shielded with an appropriate material such as lead. Exposure can be controlled by moving the patient to a safe location. When the source of gamma emission is removed or shielded, the gamma radiation exposure will also stop. Patients who were initially exposed by the emitting source may have lingering health effects from that initial exposure, but will not have additional exposure after the gamma-emitting source is removed. These patients may not benefit from decontamination procedures unless they are contaminated with other substances that need to be removed. Likewise, EMS responders will not experience gamma radiation exposure if they arrive on the scene after the discrete gamma-emitting source is removed.

It is important that ionizing radiation meters (and associated probes) used by EMS responders be selected based on the types of radiological materials with which patients could be contaminated. If radiation is suspected, a health physicist should be consulted (EPA RERT, 2007).

Relatively reliable and easy-to-use instruments are available for measuring beta and gamma forms of ionizing radiation (e.g., survey meters fitted with a Geiger-Mueller detector or "GM probe," of which a "pancake" probe is one common example). This type of instrument typically functions as a rate meter and provides a reading in the units of "counts per minute" in analog or digital form.[28] For evaluating patient contamination, EMS responders might find it helpful to have access to a rate meter with a "scaler" feature. A scaler displays an integrated digital readout for a preset sample period, selected by the operator, at a point of potential contamination (e.g., a patient's hair). The integrated digital readout is easy to compare to readings from other parts of the body or to background readings taken at a distance from the patient.

Because these probes are sensitive to gamma, x, alpha, and beta radiations, they will always detect the natural background radiation levels. Unless fully shielded, they do not read zero, even in an environment that is not radiologically contaminated. For

this reason, GM probe values are more useful for comparing contamination levels at different specific positions (i.e., comparing a point of suspected contamination to a non-contaminated point) rather than for checking radiation levels against specific fixed criteria (EPA RERT, 2007).[29] The U.S. Department of Health and Human Services' Radiological Event Medical Management Web site contains detailed information on the use of GM meters during patient contamination evaluations and other helpful guidance for providing medical services during a radiological emergency (see http://remm.nlm.nih.gov/index.html). Figure 2, at page 41, adapted from that Web site, describes how to use a radiation meter to conduct a survey for radioactive contamination on a patient or an emergency responder.

These same GM meters will detect alpha radiation to a limited extent, but are less sensitive for monitoring the presence of low-level alpha detection during decontamination procedures. When alpha radiation is present, a survey meter with an alpha scintillation probe is preferable for evaluating the alpha radiation. Alpha detectors are best used by an experienced operator under the direction of a health physicist. These professionals will also be better equipped to determine whether more than one type of radiation is present (e.g., alpha and beta, or beta and gamma).

Decontamination after a radiological materials event involves mechanical removal of the radioactive particles from the individual. The process can include washing, wiping, or irrigating the area. The decontamination team should take care not to scrub and abrade the skin. Once decontamination has been performed, the area should be resurveyed with a survey meter and appropriate probe. Decontamination efforts should continue until there is no measurable decrease in the count rate.

Chemical and Biological Agent Detection Equipment

There is no single ideal chemical or biological agent meter (or even two or three meters) that will meet all the needs of EMS responders. The requirements of this group of responders are particularly high because EMS responders have restricted space to carry equipment, are generally not hazardous sub-

---

[28] GM meters, such as the popular Ludlum Model 12 rate meter and equivalents are readily available from commercial sources and may come equipped with a range of optional features. A 900-volt model will likely be most practical for EMS responders (EPA RERT, 2007).

[29] DOE has specific criteria for fixed and removable contamination values in 10 CFR 835 Appendix D, summarized on the Lawrence Berkeley National Laboratory Web site at http://uclbl.org/ehs/orps/pdf/radContamination.pdf. The Radiological Event Medical Management Web site, http://remm.nlm.gov/remm_RadPhysics.htm#pag, lists allowable limits of radiation for the general public and radiation workers, and guidelines for radiation response worker exposure.

Figure 2. How to Do a Survey for Radiation

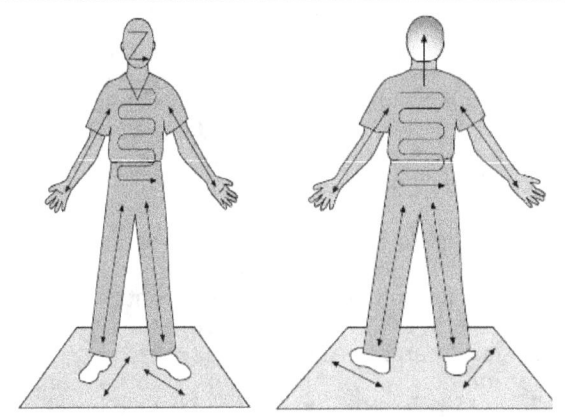

- Survey with Geiger-Mueller Detector.

  Probe held about 1/2 inch from surface.

  Move at a rate of 1 to 2 inches per second.

  Follow a systematic pattern (see above).

  Document readings in counts per minute (CPM) on a body chart.

  Compare radiation survey results before and after decontamination procedure.

- Use nuclear medicine and radiation therapy technologists or others familiar with the use of radiation detection instruments.

- Goal is < 2 times background radiation reading.

- In general, areas that register more than twice the previously determined background radiation level are considered contaminated.

- For accidents involving alpha particle emitters, if the reading is less than twice the background radiation level, the person is not contaminated to a medically significant degree. If the accident circumstances indicate that an alpha particle emitter (such as plutonium) or low-energy beta emitter could be a contaminant, a health physicist should always be consulted.

- Specifics of the survey.

  Have the person stand on a clean pad.

  Instruct the person to stand straight, feet spread slightly, arms extended with palms up and fingers straight out.

  Monitor both hands and arms; then repeat with hands and arms turned over.

  Starting at the top of the head, cover the entire body, monitoring carefully the forehead, nose, mouth, neckline, torso, knees, and ankles.

  Have the person turn around; repeat the survey on the back of the body.

  Monitor the soles of the feet.

Adapted from: USDHHS-REMM (2007) accessed September 12, 2007 at http://remm.nlm.nih.gov/howtosurvey.htm

stance technical experts, need rapid results, and may be called upon to respond to the full spectrum of hazardous substance emergencies that could occur within their community (EPA ERT, 2007). There are, however, many instruments that can contribute useful information under a variety of circumstances and may be available through local HAZMAT teams.

Promotional material, published selection criteria, and detection equipment recommendations list an increasing number of instruments available to detect and quantify hazardous substances (LSS, 2008; NIJ, 2000; IAB, 2007; HazTech, 2007; DrägerSafety, 2007; Grainger, 2007). Recent advances have lowered the detection limits of many instruments that assess airborne levels of specific chemical and biological substances. Reproducibility (of results) is also improving and the value of monitoring equipment to emergency responders is generally on the rise. Although most equipment is still more useful for evaluating an incident site and determining the presence of a hazardous substance in the environment than for declaring patients thoroughly clean after decontamination efforts, many instruments offer at least some useful information to EMS responders.

Photo-ionization detectors (PIDs) "are particularly valued by emergency responders in general for their relatively low cost, light weight, rapid detection response, and ease of use" (ILN, 2006). These detectors play an important role in the earliest phase of a response, but cannot be relied upon as the sole source of analytical information. Investigators evaluated the benefits of PID for first responders interested in detecting chemical vapors. The investigators obtained information from PID manufacturers, interviewed first responders who use these detectors, and conducted independent laboratory evaluations. The information showed that lab and user's experiences were not "always consistent with the manufacturer's stated capabilities of their equipment." As a general class of instruments, PID detectors are useful for providing rapid, suggestive (but not definitive) "information about whether a site has been compromised," but false positive readings are difficult to avoid and appropriate calibration is critical to PID effectiveness at a given site. This equipment is most useful in the initial phases of site assessment and if followed by other confirmatory test methods. Some emergency responders use PIDs for site worker health and safety support, when conditions allow (i.e., when the PID can be accurately calibrated for the specific site circumstances, the hazard is clearly identified, and in the absence of other competing substances that could cause false PID readings).

The formal report on the evaluation of PID use for first responders…

…indicates that PIDs should always be part of a decision-making context in which other qualitative and more definitive tests and instruments are used to confirm a finding. The performance of PIDs, as observed by users and quantified by independent testing, may affect the ability to make correct field decisions (ILN, 2006).[30]

Other types of detectors are also available for use with some constraints. Like PIDs, flame ionization detectors (FID) can be used primarily as a screening tool, but with verification by other evaluation methods. This is because FIDs are subject to interference by other substances and even humidity. Bulky, but still portable, (shoulder-carried) atomic absorption and gas chromatograph instruments can provide more precise and accurate levels of detection and/or chemical specificity. Although these instruments often require operators with more specialized training and need careful calibration to obtain meaningful results, HAZMAT teams using this equipment may be able to provide EMS responders with useful information on hazardous substance identification and concentration.

User-friendly equipment of adequate sensitivity is available for certain specific agents typically used as chemical weapons. HAZMAT teams in many communities have acquired a selection of handheld detection meters designed to detect parts per billion (ppb) levels of specific chemical "nerve and blister agents" used as chemical weapons (e.g., organophosphates and mustard agent) and other substances. Additionally, some of the current broad-spectrum detection devices are capable of detecting classes of agents (if not the individual agent) with reasonable sensitivity and accuracy. In some cases, other analyses of the basic properties of a substance may provide useful information about its potential to be toxic, corrosive, volatile or flammable, even when the identity or airborne concentration remain unknown (OSHA, 2006-Stakeholder Comments).

---

[30] Appendix B of the source document contains interviews with nine community incident commanders regarding the specific detection equipment they take to sites and how they use the information the detectors provide. See "Data for First Responder Use of Photoionization Detectors for Vapor Chemical Constituents" (ILN/EXT -05-00165 (Rev 1), Idaho National Laboratory (November 2006). Accessed September 4, 2007 at: www.inl.gov/technicalpublications/Documents/3589641.pdf.

EMS stakeholders who advised OSHA on this project note that the potentially small residual contaminant on clothing and skin prior to decontamination often cannot be detected efficiently with current technology. It is even more difficult to identify a handheld detection method that will assure that decontamination efforts have been adequate (except in cases of radiation release).

"There is no foolproof chemical detector and we are far from having a foolproof biological agent detector." False readings continue to be a problem, with relatively harmless chemicals triggering an alarm (OSHA Stakeholder Comments, 2006). At this time, good supervision of the washing process remains a more reliable indicator of good decontamination.

To the extent that they become available, EMS responders might also find chemical detection tapes and swabs useful for assessing the types of persistent, highly toxic, modestly volatile or non-volatile CBRNE agents that could cling to a patient's clothing, or to the patient's body once contaminated clothing has been removed (EPA ERT, 2007).

Employers of EMS responders should consider meeting with HAZMAT teams to obtain an overview of the strengths and weaknesses of the detection equipment available to the teams with which they would work in the event of an emergency release. Together they should determine the utility of these instruments to support EMS responder functions. Keep in mind that EMS responder training and powers of observation to identify cases of contamination still remain a critical element of their defense.

Methamphetamine Detection Equipment

To assist law enforcement officials who go on site during investigation or decontamination of illegal methamphetamine laboratories, NIOSH researchers have developed field methods to detect the presence of methamphetamine on surfaces, personnel and PPE. These methods will help detect the presence of the drug in illicit laboratories and evaluate the effectiveness of decontamination procedures. NIOSH reports that:

"A prominent manufacturer of sampling technologies has commercialized two low-cost, NIOSH-designed field methods to help first responders, public health officials, and remediation workers quickly detect the presence of methamphetamine on various environmental surfaces. The sampling technique can be used to detect trace levels of the illicit drug on sur-

faces, or used to evaluate decontamination efforts or clearance" (NIOSH, 2006).

The first method involves a "colorimetric test that detects the presence of methamphetamine residue on surfaces from 15 to 5000 micrograms/100 cm^2. Results should not be used for clearance purposes." The second method is a set of "semi-quantitative immunoassay tests that detect low levels of methamphetamine residue on surfaces. They may be used to determine the need for cleaning in a specific area or the need for further cleaning onsite to reach state cleanup guidelines" (SKC, 2006). The manufacturer notes that some states and counties require lab results from quantitative wipe sampling before issuing a reentry certificate after cleanup efforts. In addition to screening tests, laboratory analyses are also available.

Conclusion

These best practices are intended to help EMS responders' employers investigate and identify in advance of an incident the roles that their workers can be expected to play during a hazardous substance release event in their community (including under conditions of a mutual aid agreement). Employers should use the information in this guide when conducting hazard assessments to determine worker PPE and training needs. The hazard assessments are based in part on worker roles and on the types of hazardous substance releases for which the community is preparing. The anticipated role of workers and the related hazard assessments should help guide the employers' decisions about how to prepare their EMS responders to work as safely as is reasonably possible during treatment and transport of victims of hazardous substance releases.

In determining appropriate PPE and training for their EMS responders, employers should refer to the Summary of OSHA's Recommendations for Training and PPE section of this guide (at pg. 32).

OSHA®
Occupational Safety and
Health Administration

Appendix A

Air-purifying respirator (APR): A respirator that uses filters, cartridges, or canisters to cleanse the air.

Atmosphere supplying respirator (ASR): A respirator that provides clean air from an uncontaminated source to the facepiece. Examples include supplied-air (airline) respirators, SCBA, and combination supplied-air/SCBA.

Assigned protection factor (APF): A rating assigned to a respirator style by OSHA. This rating indicates the level of protection most workers can expect from properly worn, maintained, and fitted respirators used under actual workplace conditions. An APF of 1,000 indicates that the concentration of contaminant inside the facepiece would be 1,000 times lower than the concentration in the surrounding air. A respirator with an APF of 1,000 will provide greater protection than a respirator with an APF of 100. *(Note: The APF should not be confused with a similar measure, the "fit factor," obtained during quantitative fit testing. Fit factors, which tend to be higher numbers, provide a relative indication of how well a respirator fits an individual, but do not represent the level of protection the respirator would provide in the workplace.)*

Awareness level: See first responder awareness level.

CBRN: Chemical, biological, radiological, or nuclear [agent or substance].

CBRNE: Chemical, biological, radiological, nuclear, or explosive [agent or substance].

Cold zone: Area free of contamination. Equipment and people leaving the hot zone should be decontaminated prior to arriving at the cold zone. If a hazardous substance from patients or equipment contaminates the cold zone, the area is redefined as a warm zone.

Decontaminate (or decontamination): The process of removing hazardous substance contamination from a patient, equipment or other material. See also Gross Decontamination and Technical Decontamination.

Doff: To take off or remove (e.g., PPE).

Don: To put on, in order to wear (e.g., PPE).

EMS: Emergency medical services. The emergency medical service system can encompass all levels of patient emergency care, treatment or transport.

EMS responder: Individual trained to answer public safety requests for emergency medical care. Includes all levels of emergency medical technicians

(EMTs) and paramedics. For the purposes of this document, the term EMS responder also includes individuals cross-trained or holding multiple qualifications (e.g., firefighter, hazardous materials team member, police officer) only at the time that they are performing the duties of an EMT or paramedic.

EMT: Emergency medical technicians of all levels (EMT-Basic, EMT-Intermediate, EMT-Paramedic).

ERP: Emergency response plan.

First responder: Personnel who have responsibility to initially respond to emergencies. Some examples are firefighters, HAZMAT team members, law enforcement officers, lifeguards, forestry personnel, EMTs, and other public service personnel. In the case of hazardous materials incidents, these personnel typically respond at the site where the incident occurred.

First responder awareness level: Individuals who might reasonably be anticipated to witness or discover a hazardous substance release and who have been trained to initiate an emergency response sequence by notifying the proper authorities of the release. They would take no further action beyond notifying the authorities. [OSHA HAZWOPER Standard, 29 CFR 1910.120(q)(6)(i)].

First responder operations level: Individuals who respond to releases or potential releases of hazardous substances as part of the initial response to the site for the purpose of protecting nearby persons, property, or the environment from the effects of the release. These individuals shall have received at least 8 hours of training or have sufficient experience to objectively demonstrate competency in specific critical areas. [OSHA HAZWOPER Standard, 29 CFR 1910.120(q)(6)(ii)].

Gross decontamination: The process of removing clothing and/or a water rinsing of the naked body to quickly remove the majority of hazardous substance contamination from a patient. Also called primary, or expedient decontamination.

HAZCOM: OSHA's Hazard Communication standard [29 CFR 1910.1200].

HAZMAT: Hazardous material.

HAZWOPER: OSHA's Standard on Hazardous Waste Operations and Emergency Response, 29 CFR 1910.120. In particular, paragraph (q) of this standard covers employers whose workers are engaged in emergency response to hazardous substance releases.

Hazard response zones: Any of the three areas designated to indicate the degree of hazard and location of response activities. The three zones are hot zone, warm zone, and cold zone. Consult the glossary entry for the individual zone for a more detailed definition.

Hazard vulnerability analysis (HVA): The identification of potential emergencies and direct and indirect effects these emergencies may have on the organization's operations and the demand for its services.

Hazardous Substance: Any substance exposure to which may result in adverse effects on the health or safety of workers. This includes substances defined under Section 101(14) of CERCLA; biological or disease-causing agents that may reasonably be anticipated to cause death, disease, or other health problems; any substance listed by the U.S. Department of Transportation as hazardous material under 49 CFR 172.101 and appendices; and substances classified as *hazardous waste.*

Hazardous Substances Emergency Events Surveillance System (HSEES): A state-based system operated by the Agency for Toxic Substances and Disease Registry (ATSDR) since 1989. The system is intended to help characterize the public health consequences of hazardous substance releases. Approximately one-third of the U.S. states currently participate by collecting and submitting information. The HSEES database stores information on events, chemicals, victims, injuries and evacuations.

Hospital incident command system (HICS): An example of an optional NIMS-based ICS tailored specifically for use by hospitals and designed to function in conjunction with other common ICSs used by emergency response agencies (e.g., Fire Service Incident Command System). See Appendix I for additional information.

Hot zone: An area in and immediately surrounding a hazardous substance release. It is assumed to pose an immediate health risk to all persons, including EMS responders.

IDLH: Immediately dangerous to life or health means an atmospheric concentration of any toxic, corrosive or asphyxiant substance that poses an immediate threat to life or would interfere with an individual's ability to escape from a dangerous atmosphere. NIOSH publishes a list of IDLH concentrations for various substances. NIOSH has set the IDLH levels based on several toxicity criteria, which give priority to 30-minute acute data that demonstrates the concentration that is lethal to 50 percent of laboratory animals in 30 minutes.

Incident command system (ICS): A flexible organizational structure which provides a basic expandable system adapted by the Department of Homeland Security as the common emergency

response organizational structure throughout the nation.

Incident commander (IC): The individual who holds overall responsibility for incident response and management.

JCAHO: Joint Commission on Accreditation of Healthcare Organizations.

LEPC: Local Emergency Planning Committee.

Mass casualty: "A combination of patient numbers and patient care requirements that challenge or exceed a community's ability to provide adequate patient care using day-to-day operations" (Barbera and MacIntyre, 2003).

NFPA: National Fire Protection Association.

NHTSA: National Highway Traffic Safety Administration, an organization under the U.S. Department of Transportation (U.S. DOT).

NIMS: The National Incident Management System, established by the U.S. Department of Homeland Security as a standardized management approach to incident response, including the NIMS-based ICS, that all responders will use to coordinate and conduct response actions.

Paramedic: An Emergency Medical Technician – Paramedic level. A person who is trained to give emergency medical treatment or assist medical professionals in providing advanced life support.

Personal protective equipment (PPE): Examples include protective suits, gloves, foot covering, respiratory protection, hoods, safety glasses, goggles and face shields.

Powered air-purifying respirator (PAPR): A respirator that uses a battery-powered blower to force air through a filter or purifying cartridge before blowing the cleaned air into the respirator facepiece.

Self-contained breathing apparatus (SCBA): A respirator that provides fresh air to the facepiece from a compressed air tank (usually worn on the worker's back).

Skilled support personnel: Personnel, not necessarily an employer's own workers, who are skilled in the operation of certain equipment, such as mechanized earthmoving or digging equipment or crane and hoisting equipment, and who are needed temporarily to perform immediate emergency support work that cannot reasonably be performed in a timely fashion by an employer's own workers, and who will be or may be exposed to the hazards at an emergency response scene [from 1910.120(q)(4)].

Supplied-air respirator (SAR): A respirator that provides breathing air through an airline hose from an uncontaminated compressed air source to the face-

piece. The facepiece can be a hood, helmet, or tight fitting facepiece.

Technical decontamination: The process of using a cleansing agent to completely clean a patient. The cleansing agent is typically soap and water, but might include other solvents. Technical decontamination (also called secondary, or precautionary decontamination) is more thorough, but also more time-consuming than gross decontamination.

Triage: The process of screening and classifying sick, wounded, or injured persons to determine priority needs in order to ensure the efficient use of medical personnel, equipment and hospitals.

Warm zone: The area surrounding the hot zone, where primary contamination is not expected but where personnel must use protective clothing and equipment to avoid hazardous substance exposure from contaminated victims. People and items are decontaminated in this zone as they return from the hot zone and before being released to the cold zone. The warm zone is located between the hot zone and the cold zone, with consideration of environmental factors such as wind direction and geographic conditions.

Appendix B

References

Exposure 29 CFR 1910.120. Hazardous Waste Operations and Emergency Response standard, 29 CFR 1910.120, Code of Federal Regulations.

Adams, D. & Elliot, T. 2006. Impact of safety needle devices on occupationally acquired needlestick injuries: a four-year prospective study. Journal of Hospital Infection 64:50-55.

AHRQ. 2005. Development of models for emergency preparedness – personal protective equipment, decontamination, isolation/quarantine, and laboratory capacity (AHRQ Pub. No. 05-0099). U.S. Department of Health and Human Services, Agency for Healthcare Research and Quality (AHRQ). August. Accessed at: www.ahrq.gov/research/devmodels

ANSI/ASSE. 2006. ANSI/ASSE Z15.1 standard on Safe Practices for Motor Vehicle Operators. American National Standards Institute (ANSI) with the American Society of Safety Engineers (ASSE). February. Available at http://webstore.ansi.org/RecordDetail.aspx?sku=ANSI/ASSE%20Z15.1-2006

ATSDR. 2001. Managing Hazardous Materials Incidents (Volume 1) – Emergency Medical Services: A Planning Guide for the Management of Contaminated Patients. U.S. Department of Health and Human Services, Agency for Toxic Substances and Disease Registry (ATSDR). Accessed September 20, 2007 at: www.atsdr.cdc.gov/mhmi/#bookmark05

ATSDR. 2004. Hazardous Substances Emergency Events Surveillance (HSEES) – Annual Report 2004. U.S. Department of Health and Human Services, Agency for Toxic Substances and Disease Registry (ATSDR). Accessed September 1, 2007 at: www.atsdr.cdc.gov/HS/HSEES/annual2004.html

ATSDR. 2007. E-mail communications between ATSDR statisticians and ERG regarding "Statistician Inquiry" – HSEES database results for EMT/EMSs. U.S. Department of Health and Human Services, Agency for Toxic Substances and Disease Registry (ATSDR). August 8 and 9.

Baker et al. 2006. EMS helicopter crashes: What influences fatal outcome? Annals of Emergency Medicine 47(4). April.

Barg. 2004. Breaking down barriers: Collaborative education drives collective change. Article on Internet Web site for the Office of the Fire Marshall, Province of Ontario, Canada. October 4. Accessed February 11. www.ofm.gov.on.ca/english/FireService/announcements/2004/Breaking%20Down%20Barriers.asp

Berrios-Torres, S.I. et al. (2003). World Trade Center rescue worker injury and illness surveillance, New York, 2001. Am J Prev Med 25(2): 79-87.

Berkowitz, Z., et al. (2004). Hazardous substances releases causing fatalities and/or people transported to hospitals: rural/agricultural vs. other areas. Prehospital Disaster Med 19(3): 213-20.

Boal W.L., Hales, T., Ross, C.S. 2005. Bloodborne pathogens among firefighters and emergency medical technicians. Prehosp Emerg Care. Apr-Jun; 9(2):236-247.

Burgess, et al. 2002. Medical surveillance of clandestine drug laboratory investigators. J Occup Environ Med. 44(2):184-9 (abstract only). (February).

Caldicott, et al. 2005. Clandestine drug laboratories in Australia and the potential for harm. Australian and New Zealand Journal of Public Health 29(2):155-162.

CA EMSA. 2006. Hospital Incident Command System Guidebook. Accessed May 21, 2007 at: www.emsa.cahwnet.gov/hics/hics%20guidebook%20and%20glossary.pdf

CDC. 2003. Interim Guidelines for Hospital Response to Mass Casualties from a Radiological Incident. Centers for Disease Control and Prevention (CDC), U.S. Department of Health and Human Services. December.

Cone, D.C., McNamara R.M. 1998. Injuries to emergency medicine residents on EMS rotations. Prehosp Emerg Care. Apr-Jun; 2(2):123-6.

Cydulka, R.K., Emerman C.L., et al. 1997. Stress levels in EMS personnel: a national survey. Prehospital Disaster Med. Apr-Jun; 12(2):136-40.

DHHS. 2006. Maps of methamphetamine drug seizure. Department of Health and Human Services, www.MethResources.gov Web Site. Accessed September 4, 2006 at: www.methresources.gov/AudienceInfoTypeResult.aspx?AudId=1&InfoId=2

DrägerSafety. 2007. Fire and Emergency Services. Internet web page for DrägerSafety. Accessed September 3 at: www.draeger.com/ST/internet/US/en/index.jsp

Ellen, S. 2003. Personal Decon. Military Medical Technology – On-line Archives, 7(4) (June). Accessed September 4, 2006 at: www.military-medical-technology.com/article.cfm?DocID=130

EMS Insider, 2006. Ambulance safety gains momentum. EMS Insider, Vol. 24(6). June.

EnviroFoam. 2008. Internet Web site for EnviroFoam Technologies, Inc., Huntsville, Alabama. Accessed June 30, 2008 at: www.envirofoam.com/EasyDecon/FactSheet.aspx?ID=17

EPA-ERT. 2007. Personal communication between a representative of the U.S. Environmental Protection Agency (U.S. EPA) Emergency Response Team (ERT), Las Vegas, Nevada and ERG. August 30.

EPA RERT. 2007. Personal communication between a representative of the U.S. Environmental Protection Agency (U.S. EPA) Radiological Emergency Response Team (RERT), Las Vegas, Nevada and ERG. September 11.

E-Z-EM. 2006. What is RSDL? Internet Web site for RSDecon. E-Z-EM, Inc., Lake Success, New York. Accessed September 5 at: www.rsdecon.com

FEMA, 2007. National emergency responder credentialing – EMS job titles (FEMA 509-3). Federal Emergency Management Agency. July. Accessed September 10, 2007 at: www.fema. gov/pdf/emergency/nims/ems_jobtitle_112906.pdf

Georgopoulos, P.G., et al. 2004. Hospital response to chemical terrorism: personal protective equipment, training, and operations. American Journal of Industrial Medicine 46(5):432-445. November.

Gershon R.R., et al. 1995 Review of accidents/injuries among emergency medical services workers in Baltimore, Maryland. Prehospital Disaster Med. Jan-Mar;10(1):14-8.

Grainger. 2007. Online catalog - chemical detection equipment. Grainger, Inc. Accessed September 3 at: www.grainger.com/images/firstresponderfaxform.pdf

Green et al. 2005. Reducing vehicle crash-related EMS worker injuries through improvements in restraint system. Presentation at the XVII World Congress on Safety and Health at Work, Orlando, FL. September 18-22.

Hall, H.I., et al. 1994. "Surveillance of hazardous substance releases and related health effects." Arch Environ Health 49(1): 45-8.

Hall, H.I., et al. 1995. "Health effects related to releases of hazardous substances on the Superfund priority list." Chemosphere 31(1): 2455-61.

Hall, H.I., et al. 1996. "Public health consequences of hazardous substance releases." Toxicol Ind Health 12(2): 289-93.

HazTech Systems. 2007. Internet Web site for HazCat. HazTech Systems, Inc., Mariposa, CA. Accessed September 3 at: www.hazcat.com

Hick, J.L., et al. 2003. Protective equipment for healthcare facility decontamination personnel: regulations, risks, and recommendations. Annals of Emergency Medicine 42(3):370-380. September.

Hick, J.L. 2007. Personal communication between Dr. Hick and ERG regarding comments on the draft Best Practices Document for EMTs Exposed to Hazardous Substances. October.

HMEP. 1996. HMEP Hazardous Materials and Terrorist Incident Response Curriculum Guidelines and the companion HMEP Hazardous Materials and Terrorist Incident Prevention Curriculum Guidelines. June 5. http://search.fema.gov/search?q=+DOT+HMEP+Curriculum+Guide++&sort=date%3AD%3AL%3Ad1&output=xml_no_dtd&le=UTF-8&oe=UTF-8&client=usfa&proxystylesheet=usfa&site=usfa&btnG.x=7&btnG.y=5

Homeland Security Council. 2005. National Planning Scenarios. April. [Draft copy] accessed February 11, 2007. http://media.washingtonpost.com/wp-srv/nation/nationalsecurity/earlywarning/NationalPlanningScenariosApril2005.pdf

Horton, D.K., Berkowitz, Z., W.E. Kaye. 2003. Secondary contamination of ED personnel from hazardous materials events, 1995-2001. Am J Emerg Med 21:199-204. May.

Horton et al. 2008. Secondary contamination of medical personnel, equipment, and facilities resulting from hazardous materials events, 2003–2006. Disaster Medicine and Public Health Preparedness, 2(2):104-113.

Houser et al. 2004. Emergency Responder Injuries and Fatalities: An Analysis of Survey Data (Technical Report). Document number TR-100-NIOSH. Rand, Santa Monica, California. (March).

Hurst, C.G. 1997. Decontamination. Chapter 15 in Medical Aspects of Chemical and Biological Warfare. Published by Department of the Army, Office of The Surgeon General, Borden Institute. Accessed March 30, 2008 at: www.borden institute.army.mil/published_volumes/chem Bio/Ch15.pdf

IAB. 2007. Standardized Equipment List (SEL), InterAgency Board for Equipment Standardization and Interoperability (IAB). http://www.iab.gov/Documents.aspx

Ilhan et al. 2006. Long working hours increase the risk of sharp and needlestick injury in nurses: the need for new policy implication. Journal of Advanced Nursing 56(5):563 – 568.

"Data for First Responder Use of Photoionization Detectors for Vapor Chemical Constituents" (ILN/EXT -05-00165 (Rev 1), Idaho National Laboratory (November 2006). Accessed September 4, 2007 at: www.inl.gov/technical publications/Documents/3589641.pdf

Kahn, C.A., Pirrallo, R.G., Kuhn, E.M. 2001. Characteristics of fatal ambulance crashes in the United States: an 11-year retrospective analysis. Prehosp Emerg Care. Jul-Sep;5(3):261-9.

Kales, S.N., et al. 1997. Injuries caused by hazardous materials accidents. Ann Emerg Med 30(5): 598-603.

Kaye, W.E., M.F. Orr, et al. (2005). "Surveillance of hazardous substance emergency events: identifying areas for public health prevention." Int J Hyg Environ Health 208(1-2): 37-44.

LaTourrette, et al. 2003. Protecting Emergency Responders, Volume 2: Community views of safety and health risks and personal protection needs. Rand, Santa Monica, California. Document number MR-1646-NIOSH.

Levick, N. 2006. Hazard analysis and vehicle safety issues for emergency medical service vehicles: where is the state of the art? Session 732. Presentation at American Society of Safety Engineers Conference, Seattle, WA. June. Accessed at: www.objectivesafety.net/ LevickASSEPDC2006.pdf

LSS. 2008. Safety and Industrial Catalog 7FQ (First Edition). Laboratory Safety Supply (LSS), Janesville, WI.

Macintyre, A.G., et al. 2000. Weapons of Mass Destruction Events with Contaminated Casualties: Effective Planning for Health Care Facilities. JAMA 283(2):242-249. January 12.

Maguire, B.J., et al. 2002. Occupational Fatalities in Emergency Medical Services: A Hidden Crisis. Ann Emerg Med 40(6): 625-632.

Maguire, B.J., et al. 2005. Occupational injuries among emergency medical services personnel. Prehosp Emerg Care. Oct-Dec;9(4):405-11.

Martyny, et al. 2005. Chemical exposures associated with clandestine methamphetamine laboratories using the hypophosphorous and phosphorous flake method of production. National Jewish Medical Research Center, Division of Environmental and Occupational Health Sciences, Denver, Colorado. (September 23) Accessed September 4, 2006 at: www.njc.org/pdf/meth-hypo-cook.pdf#search=%22%22medical%20 surveillance%20of%20Clandestine%20drug%20 laboratory%20investigators%22%20Burgess% 202002%22

Mechem, C.C., et al. 2002. Injuries from assaults on paramedics and firefighters in an urban emergency medical services system. Prehosp Emerg Care. Oct-Dec;6(4):396-401.

Miller, N., Gudmestad, T., & Eisenberg, M. 2005. Development of model infectious disease protocols for fire and EMS personnel. Prehospital Emergency Care 9:326 – 332.

MMWR. 2000. Public health consequences among first responders to emergency events associated with illicit methamphetamine laboratories--selected states, 1996-1999. MMWR Morb Mortal Wkly Rep 49(45): 1021-4.

MMWR. 2003. Ambulance crash-related injuries among emergency medical services workers – United States, 1991-2002. Mortality and Morbidity Weekly Report (MMWR). 52(8):154-6. February 28. Accessed September 10, 2007 at: www.cdc.gov/mmwr/PDF/wk/mm5208.pdf

MMWR. 2005. Public health consequences from hazardous substances acutely released during rail transit--South Carolina, 2005; selected States, 1999-2004. MMWR Morb Mortal Wkly Rep 54(3): 64-7.

Mock, E.F., Wrenn K.D., et al. 1999. Anxiety levels in EMS providers: effects of violence and shifts schedules. Am J Emerg Med. Oct;17(6):509-11.

Modec. 2008. Product promotional materials on the Internet Web site for Modec, Inc., Denver, Colorado. Accessed June 30, 2008 at: www.deconsolutions.com.

Narad, R.A. 1998. An inventory of ambulance service regulatory programs in California. Prehospital Disaster Med. Jan-Mar;13(1):49-54.

NDIC. 2004. Methamphetamine Laboratory Identification and Hazards – Fast Facts – Questions and Answers, NDIC Product No. 2004-L0559-001. National Drug Intelligence Center (NDIC), U.S. Department of Justice. Accessed September 4, 2006. www.usdoj.gov/ndic/pubs7/7341/7341p.pdf

NDIC. 2006. National Drug Threat Assessment 2006 (Table 4). National Drug Intelligence Center (NDIC), U.S. Department of Justice. Accessed September 4, 2006 at: www.dea.gov/concern/18862/meth.htm

NFPA. 2007. NFPA 1994 Standard on protective ensembles for first responders to CBRN terrorism incidents. National Fire Protection Association (NFPA), Quincy, MA.

NFPA. 2008. NFPA 1852 Standard on selection, care, and maintenance of open-circuit self-contained breathing apparatus (SCBA). National Fire Protection Association (NFPA), Quincy, MA.

NHTSA. 2000. Emergency Medical Services Education Agenda for the Future – A Systems Approach (document number HS808 711). National Highway Traffic Safety Administration, U.S. Department of Transportation (U.S. DOT). July. Accessed February 11, 2007 at www.nhtsa.dot.gov/people/injury/ems/EdAgenda/final/index.html

NIJ. 2000. Guide for the Selection of Chemical Agent and Toxic Industrial Material Detection Equipment for Emergency First Responders – Volumes I & II (NIJ Guide 100-00). National Institute of Justice, U.S. Department of Justice. June. http://ncjrs.org/pdffiles1/nij/184449.pdf

NIOSH. 2006. Two NIOSH-designed methods for detecting methamphetamine now commercially available. NIOSH e-New, 4(3) (July). National Institute for Occupational Safety and Health (NIOSH), Cincinnati, OH. Accessed September 4, 2006 at: www.cdc.gov/niosh/enews/enews V4N3.html

NIOSH. 1996. Health hazard evaluation report 95-0031-2601 – University of Medicine and Dentistry of New Jersey, University Hospital, Newark, New Jersey. National Institute for Occupational Safety and Health (NIOSH), Cincinnati, OH. October.

Nishiwaki, Y., et al. 2001. Effects of sarin on the nervous system in rescue team staff members and police officers 3 years after the Tokyo subway sarin attack. Environ Health Perspect 109(11): 1169-73.

Okumura, et al. 1998. The Tokyo subway sarin attack: disaster management, Part 1: Community emergency response. Acad Emerg Med 5(6): 613-7.

Okumura, T., et al. 2003. The chemical disaster response system in Japan. Prehospital Disaster Med 18(3): 189-92.

OSHA. 1991-Borwegen. Letter of Interpretation Addressed to Mr. William Borwegen, Service Employees International Union, AFL-CIO, Re: HAZWOPER EPA and OSHA jurisdictional issues. December 18. Accessed April 6, 2004 at www.osha.gov/pls/oshaweb/owadisp.show_document?p_table=INTERPRETATIONS&p_id=20500

OSHA. 1991-McNamara. Letter of Interpretation addressed to Mr. Edward McNamara, Executive Director, Central Massachusetts Emergency Medical Systems Corporation. RE: Training requirements for emergency medical personnel. (June14) www.osha.gov/pls/oshaweb/owadisp.show_document?p_table=INTERPRETATIONS&p_id=20302

OSHA. 1992-Chapman. Letter of Interpretation addressed to The Honorable Jim Chapman, U.S. House of Representatives. RE: Background of Standards. (November 20) www.osha.gov/pls/oshaweb/owadisp.show_document?p_table=INTERPRETATIONS&p_id=20942

OSHA. 1992-Levitin. Letter of Interpretation addressed to Howard Levitin, MD. RE: Training requirements for hospital personnel involved in an emergency response of a hazardous substance. (October 27). www.osha.gov/pls/oshaweb/owadisp.show_document?p_table=INTERPRETATIONS&p_id=20911

OSHA. 1994-Bays. Letter of Interpretation addressed to Mr. Robert Bays, Sr., Huntington Laboratories, Inc. RE: Decontamination of plush carpet surface after a spill. (June 10). www.osha.gov/pls/oshaweb/owadisp.show_document?p_table=INTERPRETATIONS&p_id=21511

OSHA. 1995-Nechis. Letter of Interpretation addressed to Barry Nechis, President, Rescue Technology. RE: The OSHA Hazardous Waste

Operations and Emergency Response (HAZWOPER) regulation. (August 28) Accessed September 10, 2007 at: www.osha.gov/pls/oshaweb/owadisp.show_document?p_table=INTERPRETATIONS&p_id=21901

OSHA. 1996-Grassley. Letter of Interpretation addressed to The Honorable Charles E. Grassley, U.S. Senate. RE: Regulations for Volunteer Rescue and Ambulance Squads. (June 11) www.osha.gov/pls/oshaweb/owadisp.show_document?p_table=INTERPRETATIONS&p_id=22193

OSHA. 1997-Whittaker. Letter of Interpretation Addressed to Mr. Thomas Whittaker, New England Hospital Engineer's Society, RE: Emergency response training requirements for hospital staff. (April 25) Accessed April 6, 2004 at www.osha.gov/pls/oshaweb/owadisp.show_document?p_table=INTERPRETATIONS&p_id=22393

OSHA. 1997-Killen. Letter of Interpretation addressed to Bill Killen, Director, Navy Fire and Emergency Services. RE: Fire fighter personal protective clothing issues. (August 28) www.osha.gov/pls/oshaweb/owadisp.show_document?p_table=INTERPRETATIONS&p_id=22467

OSHA. 2001-BBP Preamble/Final Rule. Occupational Exposure to Bloodborne Pathogens; Needlestick and Other Sharps Injuries; Final Rule. Federal Register 66:5317-5325 (January 18). www.osha.gov/pls/oshaweb/owadisp.show_document?p_table=FEDERAL_REGISTER&p_id=16265

OSHA. 2002-Hayden. Letter of Interpretation addressed to CPT Kevin Hayden, Acting Commanding Officer, State of New Jersey Emergency Management Section. RE: Training and PPE requirements for hospital staff that decontaminate victims/patients. (December 2) www.osha.gov/pls/oshaweb/owadisp.show_document?p_table=INTERPRETATIONS&p_id=24523

OSHA. 2003-Bolt. Letter of Interpretation Addressed to Mike Bolt, RE: HAZWOPER training requirements for hospital staff who decontaminate chemically contaminated patients. (April 22) Accessed April 6, 2004 at www.osha.gov/pls/oshaweb/owadisp.show_document?p_table=INTERPRETATIONS&p_id=24605

OSHA. 2004-Gantt. Letter of Interpretation addressed to Mr. Ron Gantt, Trainer/consultant, Safety Compliance Management, Inc. RE: Acceptability of using computer-based (on-line) training for the HAZWOPER 40-hour classroom training. (August 16) www.osha.gov/pls/oshaweb/owadisp.show_document?p_table=INTERPRETATIONS&p_id=24985

OSHA. 2005. OSHA Best Practices for Hospital-Based First Receivers of Victims from Mass Casualty Incidents Involving the Release of Hazardous Substances. January. Accessed September 21, 2007 at: www.osha.gov/dts/osta/bestpractices/firstreceivers_hospital.pdf

OSHA. 2006-Stakeholder Comments. Comments received in response to OSHA stakeholder meeting and review of draft Best Practices Document for EMTs Exposed to Hazardous Substances.

OSHA. 2007. Pandemic Influenza Preparedness and Response Guidance for Healthcare Workers and Healthcare Employers: www.osha.gov/Publications/OSHA_pandemic_health.pdf

OSHA. 2007-CPL 02-02-073. OSHA Instruction – inspection procedures for 29 CFR 1910.120 and 1926.65, paragraph (q): Emergency Response to Hazardous Substance Release. August. Accessed September 10, 2007, at www.osha.gov/OshDoc/Directive_pdf/CPL_02-02-073.pdf

Peate, W.F. 2001. Preventing needlesticks in emergency medical system workers. J Occup Environ Med. June; 43(6):554-575.

Pennsylvania Department of Health. 2004. The national study to prevent blood exposure in paramedics preliminary results. March. Accessed June 6, 2007 at: www.dsf.health.state.pa.us/health/lib/health/ems/natl_bloodstudy.pdf

Rischitelli, G., et al. 2001. The risk of acquiring hepatitis B or C among public safety workers: A systematic review. American Journal of Preventive Medicine 20(4):299-306.

SBCCOM. 2000a. Guidelines for Responding to a Chemical Weapons Incident. Domestic Preparedness Chemical Team, U.S. Army Soldier and Biological Chemical Command (now known as the Research, Development and Engineering Command [RDECOM]). http://transit-safety.volpe.dot.gov/training/Archived/EPSSeminarReg/CD/documents/Weapons/cwirp_guidelines.pdf.

SBCCOM. 2002. Guidelines for cold weather mass decontamination during a terrorist chemical agent incident. U.S. Army Soldier Biological Chemical Command (now known as the Research, Development and Engineering

Command [RDECOM]) . (January). Accessed March 28, 2008 at: www.edgewood.army.mil/downloads/cwirp/ECBC_cwirp_cold_weather_mass_decon.pdf

SBCCOM. 2003. Guidelines for Use of Personal Protective Equipment by Law Enforcement Personnel During a Terrorist Chemical Agent Incident. U.S. Army Soldier and Biological Chemical Command (now known as the Research, Development and Engineering Command [RDECOM]). Original June 2001. Revised July 2003. http://stinet.dtic.mil/dticrev/PDFs/ada435808.pdf.

Schultz, M., Cisek, J., and Wabeke, R. 1995. Simulated exposure of hospital emergency personnel to solvent vapors and respirable dust during decontamination of chemically exposed patients. Annals of Emergency Medicine. 26(3):324-329. September.

Schwartz, R.J., Benson L., Jacobs, L.M. 1993. The prevalence of occupational injuries in EMTs in New England. Prehospital Disaster Med. Jan-Mar;8(1):45-50.

SKC. 2006. Product promotional material for MethCheck and MethAlert – "Meth residue detectives". SKC, Inc. Eighty-Four, Pennsylvania. Accessed September 4, 2006 at: www.meth-wipe.com

Umbrell, C. 2006. Tweakers, snakes, and cold medicine – health and safety during illegal drug lab cleanup. Synergist 17(1):32-36. American Industrial Hygiene Association (AIHA), Fairfax, Virginia. (January). Accessed September 4, 2006 at: www.aiha.org/1documents/PR/Synergist-Meth%20Feature-Jan%2006.pdf#search=%22NIOSH%20Methamphetamine%20PPE%22

USACHPPM. 2003a. Personal Protective Equipment Guide for Military Medical Treatment Facility Personnel Handling Casualties from Weapons of Mass Destruction and Terrorism Events (Technical Guide 275). U.S. Army Center for Health Promotion and Preventive Medicine. August. http://chppm-www.apgea.army.mil/documents/TG/TECHGUID/TG275new.pdf

USDHHS-REMM. 2007. Radiological Event Medical Management Web site. U.S. Department of Health and Human Services. Accessed September 12 at http://remm.nlm.nih.gov/index.html

USFA/IAFC. 2006. Policies and Procedures for Emergency Vehicle Safety (including model for customization). Department of Homeland Security, U.S. Fire Administration (USFA) with the International Association of Fire Chiefs (IAFC). Accessed September 10, 2007 at: www.iafc.org/displaycommon.cfm?an=1&subarticlenbr=602

Vogt, B.M. and J.H. Sorrensen. 2002. How clean is safe? Improving the effectiveness of decontamination of structures and people following chemical and biological incidents – Final Report (ORNL/TM-2002/178). Prepared by Oakridge National Laboratory for the U.S. Department of Energy. October. Accessed September 2004 at http://emc.ornl.gov/EMCWeb/EMC/PDF/How_Clean_is_Safe.pdf

Walter, F.G., et al. 2003. Hazardous materials responses in a mid-sized metropolitan area. Prehosp Emerg Care 7:214-218. Apr-Jun.

Appendix C

Inter Agency Board for Equipment Standardization and Interoperability – general information and links to related sites, such as the Responder Knowledge Base, at www.iab.gov

- InterAgency Board – Standard Equipment List (personal protective equipment) www.iab.gov/Download/sel_section1_2006.pdf

- Radiological Event Medical Management Web site, at www.remm.nlm.gov

OSHA®
Occupational Safety and
Health Administration

Appendix D

Examples of Mutual Aid Agreements and Templates

This Appendix provides three examples of mutual aid agreements and templates for agreements between service providers and communities. The example from Westchester County, NY contains a substantial amount of detail, while another example, from the Iowa Department of Public Health, is brief and to the point. Many other formats and arrangements exist and many are publicly available on the Internet (For example, conduct an Internet search using key words such as: Mutual Aid EMT; or Mutual Aid memorandum of agreement EMT)

Emergency Management Assistance Compacts (EMACs) serve a similar purpose for mutual aid between states and can help fulfill the function of mutual aid agreements. For information on intrastate mutual aid and model intrastate legislative language, see www.emacweb.org.

Westchester County, NY Mutual Aid agreement
[View at: www.westchestergov.com/emergserv/ EMS/PDF_files/mutualaidplandec03-v5.pdf]

Template for mutual aid agreement provided by the Iowa Department of Public Health (IDPH)
[View at: www.idph.state.ia.us/ems/common/pdf/ mutual_aid_agreement.pdf]

Washington State Inter-county Mutual Aid omnibus Agreement Template
[View at: http://emd.wa.gov/plans/documents/ MutualAidHandbook.pdf]

Appendix E

Case Study – How communities and industries can use the HSEES system information to reduce events (primary prevention) and inform emergency responders as part of secondary prevention (excerpt from Kaye et al. 2005).

Ammonia

Background
During 1996-2001, ammonia releases constituted 6.2% of all releases reported to HSEES. The ammonia events were also 68% more likely to result in more victims than expected based on the percentage of all events in that category. Because of the prevalence of victims during these events, ammonia releases have been targeted for prevention in many states.

Primary prevention
As part of primary prevention efforts that targeted industry, Texas offered to provide frequent spillers with their own HSEES data. A food processing company responded by requesting their spill data. From the data they discovered that two facilities they had just purchased had never reported any chemical releases to either HSEES or the Nuclear Regulatory Commission (NRC). The two facilities apparently were lax in maintaining release records [a situation that could be easily corrected].

To reduce the risk of employee exposure and minimize losses due to contaminated processed foods, this company also implemented many process safety measures in all 13 of its Texas facilities. These measures included:

- Training on good workplace safety practices for both new and veteran employees.
- Designing and implementing pollution prevention systems to capture released ammonia by way of a water recovery system, rather than create fugitive plant emissions.

The company specifically used HSEES data to evaluate the cyclic nature of ammonia (refrigerant) releases and found that there was a higher frequency of releases during the summer, when outside temperatures were greater than 100°F. Engineering controls were added to the refrigeration systems to compensate for higher seasonal pressure, thereby reducing the frequency of releases. A periodic inspection and maintenance schedule minimized component failures before they occurred. By the end of 1999, an automated early warning ammonia detection system was installed in each company processing facility.

Secondary prevention
Because of the prevalence of ammonia-related injuries, many of the states participating in the HSEES system have chosen to target the producers, transporters, and handlers of ammonia for secondary prevention of injuries. The farm belt states particularly target their prevention activities around ammonia because of the large quantities of ammonia fertilizers used. One such state is Minnesota, which analyzed its ammonia release data and produced an article aimed at health and safety personnel (Souther et al., 2000) and first responders (Souther et al., 2002). These articles contained additional information about ammonia and possible health effects from exposure, how to respond to an ammonia release safely, and first-aid tips if exposure occurs. Calls from fire departments for more information were received after the articles were published. The articles were used during training of fire department personnel, and techniques described in the article are actively used by fire department personnel when responding to ammonia releases.

**Occupational Safety and
Health Administration**

In 1989, the Agency for Toxic Substances and Disease Registry (ATSDR) implemented an active state-based hazardous substances emergency events surveillance system (HSEES) in an attempt to adequately characterize the public health consequences of hazardous substance releases. A hazardous substance emergency event (herein called "event") is defined as uncontrolled or illegal releases or threatened releases of chemicals or their hazardous by-products. The HSEES collects information on events, chemicals, victims, injuries and evacuations. Analysis of the HSEES data helps identify risk factors associated with hazardous substances releases.

A knowledge of risk factors can be useful when developing public safety interventions and can impact the guidelines and policies aimed at reducing the number of events (primary prevention) and the morbidity and mortality associated with such events (secondary prevention) (Kaye et al., 2005).

Using the HSEES system, participating states have been able to develop prevention outreach activities such as awareness training of first responders, primary prevention of spills, and secondary prevention of related injuries and deaths. One such case, involving ammonia, has been excerpted from Kaye et al. (2005) and is presented in the inset, above.

Following are several additional studies that have reviewed the HSEES system data and provide valuable trend analysis information that might help employers in planning for common incident types in their areas. These examples also further illustrate the type of information available from the HSEES system.

Evaluation of Data from the Early 1990s
Hall et al. (1994, 1995, and 1996) studied the results of events reported to the HSEES system from January 1, 1990, through December 31, 1992. General trends resulting from the reported hazardous releases are briefly summarized below.

Events
The majority (72%) of events occurred at fixed facilities (e.g., industrial sites, schools, farms, etc.) while the remaining (28%) were transportation-related (e.g., surface, air, or water transport). (Hall et al. 1994 & 1996). Spills (72%) and fires (10%) accounted for the majority of release types while the remaining events resulted from explosions and other types of releases (Hall et al., 1995). Over half (55%) of the events occurred in areas with industrial or commercial land use with an additional quarter

of events taking place in areas classified as rural (Hall et al. 1994 & 1996). Even fewer events are reported for residential areas. Most events occurred on weekdays and typically took place between the hours of 6 a.m. to 6 p.m. Fewer events occurred on the weekends.

Chemicals
In the majority of events, only one chemical was released. The most frequently released chemicals were herbicides (19%), volatile organic compounds (17%), acids (12%), and ammonias (13%) with the remaining substance categories all below 10%. (Hall et al. 1994 & 1996). In events with victims, acids, volatile organic compounds, and ammonias were most often released, while an increased number of herbicide releases occurred in transportation events.

Victims
On the whole, workers (64%) were injured more frequently than the general public (22%) or first responders (14%) (e.g., firefighters, police officers, or hazardous materials or emergency response teams) (Hall et al. 1994 & 1996). Typically in transportation-related events, fewer (10%) of the victims involved were from the general public (Hall et al. 1994 & 1996). Most events were associated with a limited number of injuries. For example, half of the events resulted in just one injured person and one quarter of the remaining events resulted in two injured people. The majority of those injured tended to be male with a mean age in the mid-thirties (Hall et al., 1994 & 1995).

Injuries
Some victims sustained more than one type of injury from an event. The most frequently reported injuries were respiratory irritation (40%) and eye irritation (27%), followed by nausea (10%) (Hall et al., 1994 & 1996). In transportation events, victims also commonly received trauma injuries and chemical burns. Injuries associated with death were trauma, chemical burns, thermal burns, heat stress, cardiac arrest and asphyxiation. Hall et al. (1994) reported that 62% of the victims, including all the victims from the general public, did not use any type of personal protective equipment. Treatment either occurred on-scene or at the hospital.

Evacuations
Evacuations were ordered for between 13-14% of the events occurring between 1990 and 1992 with a majority of the evacuations ordered by a public offi-

cial (e.g., police officer or firefighter). In-place sheltering was ordered for a few events. Hall et al. (1994) reports that in more than half of the evacuations, the evacuation zone was a circle or radius around the event, while in 21% of evacuations, no criteria was used for the evacuation zone, in 18% the zone was downwind and in 6%, the affected building or part of the building was evacuated.

Rural/agricultural area compared to all other non-rural areas

Berkowitz et al. (2004) examined data reported to the HSEES system from 1993 to 2000. These data were used to study factors associated with death/multiple victims resulting from events involving the acute release of hazardous substances in rural/agricultural areas compared to events in all other non-rural/non-agricultural areas. In particular, this analysis offers interesting insight into the extent to which local environment and activities influence the type of chemical events that occur.

Event parameters are shown in Table E-1. Berkowitz et al. (2004) evaluated 43,133 events (transportation and fixed facility) that were reported to the HSEES from 1993-2000. There were a total of 579 death/multiple victim events of which 18% took place in rural/agricultural areas while 81% took place in other non-rural areas. Death/multiple-victim events in rural/agricultural areas were more likely to be associated with transportation incidents and fires and/or explosions than in other situations. Of the transportation events in the rural/agricultural areas, 19 were associated with air transport (mainly crop dusters) and resulted in 18 deaths.

Industries associated with rural/agricultural areas included agriculture, forestry, fisheries, and manufacturing. In addition to transportation, industries involved in the other non-rural area events included manufacturing, and professional services (e.g., schools, hospitals, and nursing/personal care services).

Table E-1. HSEES Reported Event Parameters During 1993-2000

Parameters	Rural/agricultural areas	All other non-rural areas
Number of events	6,661	36,472
Total Death/multiple victim events (transportation/fixed facility)	107 (63/44)	472 (68/404)
Number of total victims	632	7,981
Number of total deaths	91	116
Most common chemical releases	The most frequently released chemicals in the rural/agricultural areas were pesticides (14%), ammonia (7.5%), and chlorine (6.5%). Multiple chemicals were involved in 18% of the total rural releases.	Events involving carbon monoxide (27%) and 0-chlorobenzylidene malononitrile (19%) (a tearing agent) were relatively common, although ammonia, chlorine, and hydrochloric acid accounted for a portion of the releases (7 to 9 percent each).
Injuries	The majority of deaths resulted from trauma (12.8%) or a combination of traumatic and other injuries (3.6%). Of those victims admitted to the hospital in rural areas, the majority presented with respiratory tract symptoms (29.4%) often accompanied by gastrointestinal symptoms (2.1%), eye irritation (0.8%), headache (1.3%), shortness of breath (<0.1%), or other symptoms.	Deaths resulted mainly from trauma (2.9%), or a combination of traumatic and other injuries (0.9%), including thermal burns (0.4%) and asphyxiation. Victims admitted to the hospital in all other areas suffered from respiratory tract symptoms (26.6%), similar to those in rural areas.
Evacuations (transportation/fixed facility)	39/107 events	350/472 events
Berkowitz et al. (2004)		

The findings presented in the studies above shed light on the trends in hazardous substance releases that occurred during the 1990s. It is important to keep in mind that these events were accidental releases, rather than intentional releases related to terrorism. Nevertheless, unintentional releases continue to be the most common cause of events related to hazardous substance releases and historical data such as from the HSEES system can be a valuable resource when identifying and evaluating the reasonably anticipated worst-case scenarios nationwide (and in local communities) as part of a hazard assessment for EMS responders. Accordingly, available relevant trends derived from such sources should be considered when evaluating EMS responder preparation (i.e., training, PPE) for these events.

Appendix F

Special Considerations for Responses Involving Methamphetamine Laboratories

Public health officials increasingly recognize clandestine methamphetamine laboratories as a hazard to first responders, including EMS personnel. Overall reports of injuries are substantially more common for incidents involving these laboratories than for hazardous substance release incidents in general (MMWR, November 17, 2000).[31] Furthermore, the incidence of methamphetamine use, associated emergency room visits, lab seizures, and related incidents have increased dramatically over the past decade, both in the U.S. and internationally (see Table F-1 and Figure F-1) (NIDC, 2006; Caldicott, 2005; DHHS, 2006). Due to the clandestine nature of these scenes, occupants are not usually forthcoming about the conditions when they report an emergency. All too often the labs are identified in the line of duty by responders who are not wearing any personal protective equipment (PPE) (Caldicott, 2005). First responders may have no warning that a hazardous substance release has occurred or is in progress when they arrive.

> OSHA is preparing a helpful guide addressing cleanup work at clandestine methamphetamine laboratories. Until the guide is available, this appendix offers background information relevant to EMS personnel responding to this type of scene.

Table F-1. Reported Methamphetamine Laboratory Seizures, 1997-2005

Year	Total Laboratories	Superlabs *
1997	2,806	**
1998	3,802	**
1999	6,750	**
2000	7,021	**
2001	8,542	245
2002	9,282	142
2003	10,199	130
2004	9,895	55
2005***	5,249	37

Adapted from NIDC, 2006. Data source: El Paso Intelligence Center National Clandestine Laboratory Seizure System.

*Large-scale production facilities that produce 10 pounds or more of drug per production cycle (NDIC, 2004), which typically excludes small-scale "apartment" or "backpack" labs.

**Laboratory capacity data were not collected prior to 2001.

*** Data for 2005 are preliminary.

---

[31] Injuries were associated with 52.7 percent of HSEES-reported incidents involving clandestine methamphetamine laboratories. By comparison, injuries were reported for 7.2 percent of all hazardous substance incidents entered in HSEES (MMWR, November 17, 2000).

Figure F-1. Distribution of U.S. Clandestine Methamphetamine Lab Incidents by State – 2004

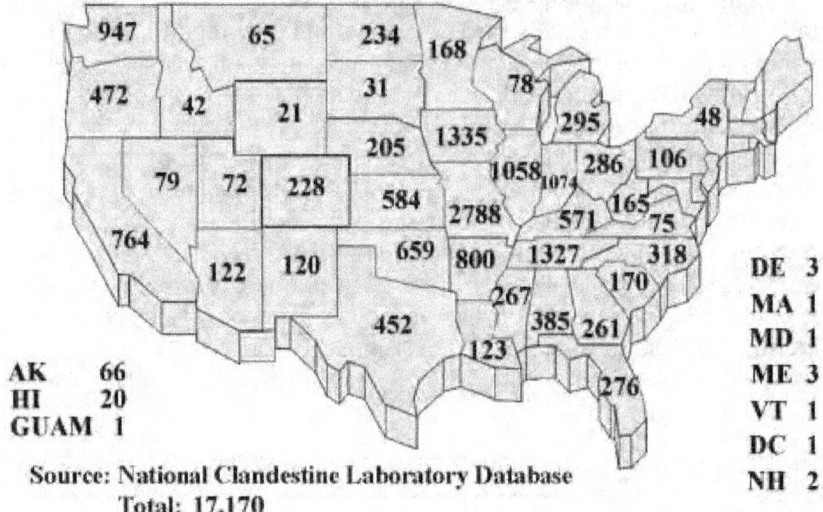

Total of All Meth Clandestine Laboratory Incidents
Including Labs, Dumpsites, Chem/Glass/Equipment
Calendar Year 2004

Source: National Clandestine Laboratory Database
Total: 17,170

map last updated on August 18, 2005

Source: DHHS, 2006

EMS responders can be counted among the victims of clandestine methamphetamine lab incidents. MMWR (2000) reported an incident in April 1996, where three Washington State EMTs and two police officers experienced eye and respiratory irritation after being exposed to emissions from a fire involving acetone, hydrochloric acid, and sodium hydroxide in an illicit methamphetamine lab in an apartment. Furthermore, EMS responders were among the victims reported to the HSEES system by the five states that contributed hazardous substance release data specifically associated with methamphetamine laboratories between 1996 and 1999 (MMWR, 2000). These data included eight cases of respiratory tract irritation among EMS responders (47.1 percent of all symptoms reported by EMS responders during methamphetamine laboratory incidents), four cases of eye irritation (23.5 percent), two cases of nausea and vomiting (11.8 percent), and one report each of skin irritation, headache, and shortness of breath (each 5.9 percent) (see Table F-2). EMS responders sustained most injuries through on-site exposure or direct contact with the clothing or skin of contaminated persons. None of the injured first responders were wearing PPE at the time of injury (MMWR, November 17, 2000).

Table F-2. Number and Percentages of First Responders Who Sustained Injuries during Emergency Events Associated with Illicit Methamphetamine Laboratories by Type of Injury

Injury*	Firefighters No.	Firefighters %	Police Officers No.	Police Officers %	EMTs No.	EMTs %	Hospital Personnel No.	Hospital Personnel %	Total No.	Total %
Trauma	1	12.5	0	-	0	-	0	-	1	0.9
Respiratory irritation	3	37.5	49	62.0	8	47.1	0	-	60	54.1
Eye irritation	0	-	8	10.1	4	23.5	0	-	12	10.8
Nausea/vomiting	0	-	4	5.1	2	11.8	3	42.9	9	8.1
Heat stress	0	-	1	1.3	0	-	0	-	1	0.9
Chemical burns	3	37.5	0	-	0	-	0	-	3	2.7
Skin irritation	0	-	0	-	1	5.9	0	-	1	0.9
Dizziness/CNS	0	-	6	7.6	0	-	4	57.1	10	9.0
Headache	0	-	2	2.5	1	5.9	0	-	3	2.7
Shortness of breath	0	-	9	11.4	1	5.9	0	-	10	9.0
Other	1	12.5	0	-	0	-	0	-	1	0.9
Total	8	100	79	100	17	100	7	100	111	100

Source: MMWR, 2000 (based on HSEES system data 1996-1999 from five reporting states).
*Injuries include illnesses and other adverse health effects.

Methamphetamine laboratories can contain a wide variety of flammable, toxic, and/or explosive chemicals (see Table F-3). Industrial hygiene advisors also warn that clandestine laboratories can produce more than one illicit substance (Umbrell, 2006). The materials on hand might represent those needed for a variety of drug "products." Drug makers sometimes also stockpile quantities of ingredients, so large amounts of these dangerous substances can be present.

Table F-3. Chemical Hazards Encountered at Methamphetamine Laboratories

Chemical	Hazards
Pseudoephedrine	Ingestion of doses greater than 240 mg causes hypertension, arrhythmia, anxiety, dizziness, and vomiting. Ingestion of doses greater than 600 mg can lead to renal failure and seizures.
Acetone/ethyl alcohol	Extremely flammable, posing a fire risk in and around the laboratory. Inhalation or ingestion of these solvents causes severe gastric irritation, narcosis, or coma.
Freon	Inhalation can cause sudden cardiac arrest or severe lung damage.
Anhydrous ammonia	A colorless gas with pungent, suffocating odor. Inhalation causes edema of the respiratory tract and asphyxia. Contact with vapors damages eyes and mucous membranes.
Red phosphorus	May explode as a result of contact or friction. Ignites if heated above 260°C. Vapor from ignited phosphorus severely irritates the nose, throat, lungs, and eyes.
Hypophosphorous acid	Extremely dangerous substitute for red phosphorus. If overheated, deadly phosphine gas is released. Poses a serious fire and explosion hazard.
Lithium metal	Extremely caustic to all body tissues. Reacts violently with water and poses a fire or explosion hazard.
Hydriodic acid	A corrosive acid with vapors that are irritating to the respiratory system, eyes, and skin. If ingested, causes severe internal irritation and damage that may cause death.
Iodine crystals	Gives off vapor that is irritating to respiratory system and eyes. Solid form irritates the eyes and may burn skin. If ingested, causes severe internal damage.
Phenylpropanolamine	Ingestion of doses greater than 75 mg causes hypertension, arrhythmia, anxiety, and dizziness. Quantities greater than 300 mg can lead to renal failure, seizures, stroke, and death.
Source: DEA Office of Diversion Control (NDIC, 2004).	

These substances and additional compounds, such as the phosphine gas and hydrogen chloride emitted when they are mixed or heated, present serious hazards to the skin, eyes, respiratory tract, central nervous system (CNS), and various target organs.

Neither medical surveillance nor occupational exposure results are available for EMS responders exposed to hazardous substances during clandestine drug lab response. Limited information, however, is available for other responders in related situations. Burgess et al. (2002) evaluated annual medical surveillance records for the period 1991 to 1998 for 40 California law enforcement drug laboratory investigators (methamphetamine laboratories account for most drug laboratory investigations.) During the investigations, the officers understood the hazards of the situation they would encounter and sometimes took precautions such as wearing respiratory protection, but also typically spent a considerably longer period of time in the laboratories than would an EMS responder responding to an emergency.

The study results found a median annual decline of 40 milliliters (ml) per year in the officers' lung function (average 64 ±138 ml/year), measured as forced expiratory volume in 1 second (FEV1). "For 34 subjects with valid exposure data, longer duration use of respiratory protection was associated with a less rapid decline in FEV1, whereas lack of respiratory protection during the processing phase of laboratory investigation was associated with a more rapid annual decline." The authors recommended "more assiduous use of respiratory protection" (Burgess et al., 2002). Results of blood tests administered as part of routine medical surveillance suggest no significant longitudinal changes in parameters, including serum alanine aminotransferase, serum aspartate aminotransferase, hemoglobin, and white cell count, "although platelets declined slightly."

Other investigators in Colorado noted a lack of

information about airborne concentrations of hazardous substances in active methamphetamine laboratories. This type of exposure information is necessary to ensure that first responders are adequately protected when they enter such an environment. As a step toward characterizing the potential for exposure, the researchers conducted extensive industrial hygiene area and personal air monitoring during controlled drug "cooking" experiments. For this experiment, the two "cooks," both forensic chemists, used two different, but common, methamphetamine production methods. One cook used hypophosphorous, while the other used flake phosphorous, both of which are substitutes for red phosphorus (typical of another common method). The researchers also obtained wipe samples used to evaluate the extent to which hazardous substances were deposited on surfaces. These experiments were conducted in realistic settings: the bathroom and living area of condemned structures similar to those often used as drug laboratories (Martyny et al., 2005).

The results of these tests showed that short-term exposure levels to hazardous substances in a functioning methamphetamine laboratory can be elevated to a level that can cause acute and chronic health effects. Although personal exposure levels were not typically in the IDLH range, short-term phosphine levels as high as 62.3 ppm were recorded in the immediate cooking area (on the table). This exceeds the IDLH for phosphine of 50 ppm. Furthermore, Individuals who have been "cooking" methamphetamine can carry significant surface contamination. The findings also indicate that surfaces throughout the structure can be contaminated with methamphetamine even after a single cooking cycle (Martyny et al., 2005).

Based on their sampling results, Martyny et al. (2005) offered several conclusions relevant to EMS responders responding to the scene involving a methamphetamine laboratory. These are quoted here:

- "If a methamphetamine cook is being conducted and the hypophosphorous manufacturing method is used, then exposure to levels of hydrogen chloride that exceed current occupational levels are likely.

- During the cook, it is possible that exposures to hydrogen chloride will exceed levels considered by NIOSH to be immediately dangerous to life or health (IDLH).

- Regardless of whether a cook is being conducted at the time of entry, it is likely that most items and individuals in the vicinity of the cook will be contaminated with methamphetamine.

- If a methamphetamine cook has been conducted within a building, chemicals from the cook will have spread not only in the specific area of the cook but throughout the building. This is especially true of hydrogen chloride and methamphetamine.

- If a methamphetamine cook has been conducted within a building, all children within that building are likely to have been exposed to methamphetamine and other chemicals and should be considered as exposed and contaminated.

- If any law enforcement or emergency services personnel are to be entering a building suspected of being a clandestine methamphetamine laboratory, they should enter only with self-contained breathing apparatus and complete skin protection unless it is known that the lab has not been in recent operation and that all of the chemicals are under control. In the opinion of the authors, it is not likely that these conditions will be known prior to entry in most cases. We therefore suggest that all initial entries be made with the PPE previously mentioned.

- After the suspected laboratory is known to be out of operation and the chemicals are in a stable condition, then investigators could reduce the respiratory protection portion of the PPE to a full-face air-purifying respirator with organic vapor, acid gas, and P100 combination cartridges.

- All law enforcement officers and emergency services personnel should be made aware of the high potential for exposure to methamphetamine contamination and trained in the methods to reduce the "take home" levels of methamphetamine. Testing at the scene on a periodic basis should be used to verify that personnel are not being contaminated on-scene.

- Decontamination of all items taken out of the suspected laboratory should be conducted. Efforts should be made to reduce contamination transfer outside of the laboratory and periodic testing should be conducted to assure that personnel and items are being adequately decontaminated."

Appendix G

 **Emergency Management and Response
Information Sharing and Analysis Center**

CIP BULLETIN 2-07   **February 27, 2007**

NOTE: *CIP Bulletins will be distributed as necessary to provide members of the Emergency Services Sector with timely, important, unclassified information potentially affecting the protection of their critical infrastructures. They are prepared by the Emergency Management and Response- Information Sharing and Analysis Center (EMR-ISAC) at (301) 447-1325 or by e-mail at emr-isac@dhs.gov.*

Clandestine Drug Labs
FIRST RESPONDER AWARENESS CARD

It is important to remember that every year in the United States, first responders are exposed and injured in Clandestine Drug Lab settings.

DISPATCH AND RESPONSE PHASE

- Nature of the call and location are important. When responding get all the dispatch information available via pager, cell phone or MDT (mobile data terminal). DO NOT discuss over radio if possible.
- Do any current operations or intelligence identify the location as a confirmed or possible clandestine drug lab?

ROUTINE OPERATIONS

- If you discover a lab during routine operations—GET OUT!
- Do not touch, move or handle anything.
- If you, another responder or civilians have become contaminated, immediately begin decontamination.
- **Responders should be very cautious of any materials or locations that arouse your curiosity.**

ARRIVAL ON SCENE

- If responding to a suspected or confirmed lab slow down when approaching the incident and conduct a 360-degree scan during your "windshield survey" of the scene.
- Look for objects and people that seem out of place for the location or time of the call—if it looks suspicious it probably is.
- Use Staging Area to limit number of responders initially.
- Establish an outer perimeter and remember it is also a crime scene.

**Occupational Safety and
Health Administration**

APPROACHING THE AREA

- Utilize Incident Command System (ICS) and only the necessary components for that response. (e.g., Unified Command, Safety Officer, etc.)
- Establish hazard Control Zones around the suspected lab (Hot, Warm, Cold). Limit the number of responders entering the Hot Zone.
- **Use caution when dealing with meth cooks or meth users.**
- **Be aware of the possibility of booby traps or explosive materials.**

RESPONDERS SHOULD BE VERY CAUTIOUS OF ANY ITEMS OR LOCATIONS THAT AROUSE YOUR CURIOSITY!

Clandestine Drug Labs can be discovered during an emergency response or will most likely be discovered when conducting routine response activities. Drug Labs have been found in different locations such as houses, attics, basements, apartments, storage units, barns, vehicles, campsites, confined spaces and other locations.

IDENTIFICATION

- **Responders should be very cautious of any materials or locations that arouse your curiosity.**
- Be aware of unusual structures or equipment.
- Accumulations of waste inside or outside.
- Attempted fortification or camouflaging of a location.
- Strong or unusual chemical odors inside or outside.
- Unusual or erratic behavior of individuals at location or in vicinity.
- Large amounts of Ephedrine or Pseudoephedrine.
- Plastic or glass containers containing multi-layered liquids (photo below).
- Heating units such hot plates, frying pans or pressure cookers.
- Laboratory type equipment, funnels, vessels or glassware (photo below).
- Compressed gas cylinders with unusual discoloration or attachments.
- Large or unusual amounts of household chemicals or materials.
- **ANY COMBINATION OF THE ABOVE DESCRIBED ITEMS!**

EXIT STRATEGY

- If there are several strong indicators that you have a clandestine drug lab—leave the area and withdraw your personnel to an area outside the Warm Zone.
- Call for Clandestine Drug Lab Teams and/or law enforcement assistance.

Response sheet is for training and informational purposes only. Please utilize local guidelines and procedures.

Appendix H

Training Curricula for EMS Responders

Background

The National Highway Traffic Safety Administration (NHTSA) curricula for EMS responders introduces some topics relevant to HAZWOPER first responder training. As noted in Appendix P, however, (see discussion of the roles of NHTSA and states in EMS responder training), that curricula does not in itself meet OSHA's requirements because it lacks information on relevant local community conditions. Furthermore, depending on how the NHTSA curriculum is offered, it might not meet the required 8-hour HAZWOPER training duration for first responder operations level.

The National Fire Protection Association (NFPA) offers an extensive list of competencies that supplement OSHA's requirements for EMS responders' HAZWOPER training at the first responder awareness and operations levels (as well as higher levels). Specifically, the non-regulatory NFPA 472 provides detailed recommendations for competencies NFPA believes are important for all first responders (e.g., firefighters, police, EMS) who work at the awareness or operations levels (NFPA-742, 2008). A companion standard (also non-regulatory), NFPA 473, suggests additional areas of competence specifically tailored for EMS personnel (NFPA-473, 2008).

> Two non-regulatory (optional) NFPA standards suggest training topics that can be included in HAZWOPER training for EMS responders. These two standards are:
> - NFPA 472 *Standard for Competence of Responders to Hazardous Materials/Weapons of Mass Destruction Incidents* (2008)
> - NFPA 473 *Standard for Competence for EMS Personnel Responding to Hazardous Materials/Weapons of Mass Destruction Incidents* (2008)

OSHA says of these and other NFPA standards (such as NFPA 471 – *Recommended Practice for Responding to Hazardous Material Incidents*):

In general, employers of emergency response organizations who follow the NFPA standards should be in compliance with 29 CFR 1910.120(q). It is important that the applicable portions of all related standards be followed. (OSHA, 2007-CPL-02-02-073).

As an example, OSHA notes that NFPA 471 no longer addresses the position of "safety officer," although another NFPA standard (NFPA 1500 – Standard on Fire Department Occupational Safety and Health Program) does. A designated safety officer, however, is mandatory in the HAZWOPER standard. OSHA would consider the absence of a safety officer as a failure to comply with the standard *(OSHA, 2007-CPL-02-02-073)*. Employers who use NFPA standards are ultimately responsible for ensuring that they are providing training or allowing employees to demonstrate competence that meets OSHA's requirements.

The following sections provide an outline of some of the competencies presented in NFPA 472 and NFPA 473 that are most relevant to EMS responders. Each competency includes a brief summary of how responder competence is evaluated. In general, although not precisely aligned with OSHA's competencies for first responders at the awareness and operations levels, an EMS responder that demonstrated competence in each of the areas listed by NFPA would likely also in the process demonstrate OSHA's required competencies, as long as the scenarios used for discussion are provided with the HAZWOPER competencies in mind. Consult the NFPA's standards for complete listings of the individual competencies and specific details of NFPA's recommendations for demonstrating competence.

Select Examples of Core Competencies for First Responder Awareness Level Personnel Recommended in NFPA 472:

Detecting the presence of hazardous materials (responder is requested to identify situations where hazardous materials are present, provide numerous examples of hazardous materials categories, identify specific types of container marking; perform exercises involving material safety data sheets (MSDSs) and shipping papers, and identify indicators of possible criminal activity relating to various types of hazardous substances or sites).

Surveying hazardous materials and collecting related information (responder is requested to name hazardous materials described in example incidents, describe methods for determining substance names, and look up information in a standard reference book).

Initiating protective actions (responder is requested to identify basic information from scenarios and plans, including the role of individuals at first responder awareness level, appropriate precautions and PPE (from given lists), and security measures).

Initiating the notification process (responder is requested to identify details related to notification in provided scenarios).

Select Examples of Core Competencies for First Responder Operations Level Personnel Recommended in NFPA 472:

Competencies listed for first responder awareness level personnel.

Surveying hazardous material incidents (responder is requested to discuss hazardous materials containers/packaging, possible materials release and site conditions for example scenarios, and from provided lists pick the correct answers to related questions).

Describing response objectives and identifying actions (responder is requested to describe exposures that could be avoided and risks to responders under different scenarios or for different hazard classes).

Determine suitability of PPE and decontamination issues (responder is requested to decide whether available PPE is adequate for example situations, describe various SCBA and protective clothing configurations, and exhibit knowledge about decontamination methods, equipment, and issues).

Scene control and preserving evidence (responder is requested to identify criteria and techniques for establishing scene control, allowing personnel to work, and preserving evidence under various incident site conditions).

Initiating the ICS (responder is requested to demonstrate ICS initiation for a given scenario's ERP and identify various elements of an ICS).

Using PPE (responder is requested to identify or discuss various factors that are critical to correctly using PPE, such as when to use a buddy system, control of thermal stress, and how to clean and inspect PPE).

Select Examples of Competencies for Basic Life Support and Advanced Life Support Personnel Recommended in NFPA 473:

The non-regulatory NFPA 473 is intended for "EMS personnel who respond to incidents involving hazardous materials or weapons of mass destruction." NFPA 473 also assumes that these EMS responders "are trained to meet at least the core competencies of the operations level responders" as presented in NFPA 472 (NFPA-473, 2008). It is understood that in any area of competence involving direct patient care, the EMS responder's activities must be within the scope of practice and training of the individual responder.

NFPA 473 is aligned along EMS responder quali-

fications to provide basic life support (BLS) or advanced life support (ALS), rather than along first responder awareness or operations level training requirements. Some employers might link BLS and ALS qualifications to workers roles requiring first responder operations level training and first responder awareness level training, respectively. Other employers, however, might designate worker roles along different lines, depending on conditions in the community and the employers' response plans. Although most NFPA 473 competencies for both BLS and ALS personnel are similar (or identical), there are a few differences and these are indicated by an asterisk (*) and notation summarizing the difference.

The following summary provides a number of examples of the types of competencies included in NFPA 473 specifically for EMS responders. Again, consult the NFPA's standards for complete listings of the individual competencies and specific details of NFPA's recommendations for demonstrating competence.

Surveying hazardous materials incidents (responder is requested to describe details of identification, spread of contamination, effects or treatment for a range of physical, chemical and biological hazard types). [*ALS responder is also asked to discuss how site and patients should be observed for signs of exposure.][32]

Collecting and interpreting hazard and response information (responder is requested to discuss methods for gathering information about an incident and the health effects of any hazardous materials involved). [*ALS responder is also asked to identify ways to determine whether secondary devices or other hazards might be present at the scene.]

Identifying high risk areas for potential exposures (responder is requested to assimilate given information from a variety of sources and determine areas where exposure is likely to occur.)

Incident communications (responder is requested to identify effective ways to communicate in support of the response plan).

Role of the BLS level responder [*or ALS level responder] (responder is requested to describe the ICS and how EMS responders function in performing specific duties within the system).

Determining the nature of the incident and providing medical care (responder is requested to discuss various modes and effects on patients of hazardous substance exposure during incidents). [*ALS

---

[32] An asterisk (*) indicates a notable difference in this competency for BLS responders compared to what is expected of ALS responders.

responder is expected to determine the physical and toxicological/symptomatic characteristics of substances to which a patient could be exposed.]

Decontamination (responder is requested to determine or identify specific aspects of decontamination procedures presented in a model plan and associated standard operating procedures (SOPs). [*ALS responder is expected to be able to execute specific tasks that form major components of the decontamination phase of a sample ERP and associated SOPs, for individual and mass decontamination scenarios.]

Preserving evidence (responder is requested to determine whether criminal acts are involved in example incidents and identify ways of safeguarding evidence while providing medical care).

Medical support for incidents (responder is requested to describe or demonstrate how to create and execute various aspects of a medical monitoring plan for responders wearing PPE). [*ALS responder is asked to do the same for responders wearing chemical protective suits.]

Tips for Successful EMS Responder HAZWOPER Training Programs

Successful first responder training at the awareness and operations levels depends on effective curricula and on teaching methods that are compatible with adult learners who are probably not accustomed to spending time in a classroom.

One technique for drafting a successful training program involves starting by outlining lectures and exercises that will provide participants with the tools they need to successfully "demonstrate competency" to perform the expected job functions safely and effectively. Once the curricula addresses those needs, details about laws, standards, and regulatory requirements can be incorporated into the training program where they are most relevant.

Experienced trainers keep students engaged in learning by organizing the curricula to alternate lecture periods and hands-on practical sessions. Sometimes this means that some basic information needs to be shifted later in the course to allow a hands-on skill-development session (e.g., PPE use) to be inserted between lecture sessions. Instructors can help improve the learning experience by tailoring course material so it is related to participants' work and life experience. The more interactive the course, the more easily students will learn.

OSHA permits EMS responders who receive first responder training (or demonstration of competence) at the awareness level to count it towards the operations level training requirements. This means that an employer may be able to offer just one class, with the first responder awareness level students attending only the first portion of the class.

OSHA allows flexibility in how EMS responders complete the initial and annual refresher training requirements. Those who are able to satisfy part or all of their HAZWOPER training requirement by demonstrating competence may be offered opportunities to do so as part of organized training session, drills, and exercises. OSHA also allows workers who participate in critiques after incidents to count that experience toward their training.

OSHA®
Occupational Safety and
Health Administration

Appendix I

Hospital Incident Command System

Employers of EMS responders must work closely with hospitals and other organizations during a hazardous substance release that affects patients. The employers should be familiar with incident command system structures used in their communities, including the Hospital Incident Command System (HICS) updated from the earlier version (hospital emergency incident command system – HEICS) in 2006. HICS is published by the California Emergency Medical Services Authority (EMSA). The following excerpt from the HICS Guidebook is provided as an introduction to this 2006 version and is followed by HICS Section 4.7.2 – Fire and Emergency Medical Services.

Excerpt from Hospital Incident Command System Guidebook:

Forward

Hospitals throughout the United States confront a myriad of operational and fiscal challenges on a daily basis. To effectively manage emergencies, whether external (e.g., fires, earthquakes) or internal (e.g., child abductions, utility failure), hospitals must invest the time and necessary funds to ensure adequate preparations are in place. Recent events such as the September 11, 2001 terrorism attacks, the Severe Acute Respiratory Syndrome (SARS) outbreak in 2004, and the Gulf Coast hurricanes of 2006 demonstrated the importance of hospital preplanning and personnel training.

Since its inception in the late 1980s, the Hospital Emergency Incident Command System (HEICS) served as an important emergency management foundation for hospitals in the United States. We recognized the value and importance of using an incident management system, not only in emergency situations but also in daily operations, preplanned events, and non-emergent situations. Therefore, the HEICS IV Project, sponsored by the California Emergency Medical Services Authority, has evolved to become HICS—the Hospital Incident Command System— a comprehensive incident management system intended for use in both emergent and non-emergent situations.

The HEICS IV project is not intended to be the only answer to a hospital's emergency preparedness needs. However, we believe this Guidebook and the accompanying materials can play a major role in advancing institutional preparedness while providing needed local, state, and national standardization of hospital emergency response and recovery.

We believe the new Hospital Incident Command System has built upon the benefits and successes of the original HEICS and provides hospitals of all sizes with tools needed to advance their emergency preparedness and response capability—both individually and as a member of the broader response community.

Fire and Emergency Medical Services - Section 4.7.2

Fire departments, private ambulance providers, air medical services, and a governing Emergency Medical Services (EMS) entity all have significant roles and interface with hospitals in the United States.

Fire departments provide any or all of the following services: first responder basic life support (BLS) and/or advance life support (ALS) medical care; ambulance transport; hazmat response; and search and rescue.

Private ambulance companies provide BLS and/or ALS transport for 911 responses; interfacility transports; and standby for prescheduled events, hazmat events, or search and rescue events.

EMS governing entities (which may be fire departments) provide medical direction to prehospital emergency medical technicians (EMTs) and paramedics and system oversight for all ambulance activities, to include licensure, inspection, and approval or agreement for operating areas. The medical oversight often extends to the interface between pre-hospital and hospital EMS, and in many communities this entity acts as the disaster coordinator/manager in a large-scale emergency.

Hospitals should also be familiar with air medical services that may be used and have an individual or community plan for how best to coordinate multiple requests for assistance. Planning consideration should be given to how helicopters or fixed wing aircraft can assist with personnel, patient, and equipment/supply transport if necessary.

During an emergency, EMS (which we define as the combination of any of the services described above) can be expected to bring a significant segment of the involved population to the hospital for medical care. For this reason, information-sharing procedures must be well known by both parties, and dependable and redundant communication systems and technology must be in place and properly used.

Hospitals should also be familiar with their community multiple/mass casualty plan, including appropriate response codes and terminology, as well as the triage, treatment, and transportation practices to be employed. EMS personnel should have a fundamental understanding of how the hospital will respond, including what information is needed to declare a disaster, alternative travel routes into the facility, and where triage and decontamination will be conducted.

Preplanning should also address issues such as what personnel supplementation can be provided by either party, including trained decontamination team supplementation, and how response information will be shared. In addition to patient transport and possible staff and equipment augmentation, EMS responds when the hospital itself is the scene of an incident; plans for such response should also be mutually developed.

More Information:

More information on the Hospital Incident Command System can be found at www.emsa. ca.gov/HICS/default.asp (accessed July 10, 2009).

OSHA®
Occupational Safety and
Health Administration

Appendix J

Summary of Respirator Types and
Selection Information

Summary of Respirator Types
and Characteristics

Table J-1. Summary of Respirator Types and Characteristics

Inlet covering - Every respirator has an inlet covering the part of the respirator between the user's respiratory tract and the air-purifying device or breathing air source. Inlet covering types and examples include:				
Tight-fitting • Quarter mask • Half facepiece • Full facepiece • Mouthbit/nose clamp				Loose-fitting • Hood • Helmet • Loose-fitting facepiece
Respirator types	**Typical inlet covering**	**Details**		**Example(s)**
Air Purifying				
Filtering facepieces	Tight-fitting	As user inhales, air passes through a facepiece made of filter material.		• Dust masks
Air purifying respirators (APR)	Tight-fitting	As user inhales, air passes through air-cleaning filters, cartridges, or canisters.		• Half or full facepiece respirator with particulate filters (non-powered)
Powered air purifying respirators (PAPR)	Tight or loose-fitting	A fan passes air through air-cleaning filters or cartridges.		• Full facepiece PAPR
Air-supplied				
Atmosphere supplying respirators (ASR)	Tight or loose-fitting	Supplies air from a source independent of the ambient atmosphere (e.g., via an airline or using a compressed gas tank containing an acceptable quality of breathing air (Grade D). A regulator controls the rate at which air flows to the inlet covering.		• Supplied air respirator (SAR), also called an airline respirator • Self-contained breathing apparatus (SCBA)
Escape				
Can be either negative or positive pressure and either APR or ASR	Tight or loose-fitting	• May use an air cleaning device or provide air from a small compressed gas tank (bottle). • Usually single use. • Any respirator intended to be used only for emergency exit.		• Emergency life support apparatus (ELSA) • Mouthbit

Advantages and Disadvantages of Various Types of Respiratory Protection

Table J-2. Advantages and Disadvantages of Various Types of Respiratory Protection

Type of Respirator	Advantages	Disadvantages
Air Purifying *Air-purifying respirator* (including powered air-purifying respirators (PAPR))	• Enhanced mobility • Lighter in weight than SCBA; generally weights 2 pounds or less (except for PAPRs)	• Cannot be used in IDLH or oxygen-deficient atmospheres (less than 19.5 percent oxygen at sea level). • Limited duration of protection; may be hard to gauge safe operating time in field conditions. • Only protects against specific chemicals and up to specific concentrations (see later section on Assigned Protection Factors). • Use requires monitoring of contaminant and oxygen levels. • Can only be used for specific gases or vapors provided that a cartridge change schedule is identified and a safety factor is applied, or if the unit has an ESLI (end-of-service-life-indicator).
Atmosphere-Supplying *Self-contained breathing apparatus (SCBA)*	• Provides the highest available level of protection against airborne contaminants and oxygen deficiency. • Provides the highest available level of protection.	• Bulky, heavy (up to 35 pounds). • Finite air supply limits work duration. • May impair movement in confined spaces.
Positive pressure supplied-air respirator (SAR) (also called airline respirator)	• Enables longer work periods than an SCBA • Less bulky and heavy than an SCBA; SAR equipment weigh less than 5 pounds (or 15 pounds, if escape SCBA protection is included) • Protects against most airborne contaminants	• Not approved for use in IDLH or oxygen-deficient atmospheres (less than 19.5 percent oxygen) unless equipped with an auxiliary self-contained air supply. • Impairs mobility. • NIOSH certification limits hose length to 300 feet. • As the length of the hose is increased, the airflow must be increased to ensure that the minimum approved airflow is delivered at the faceplate. • Air line is vulnerable to damage, chemical contamination, and degradation. Decontamination of hoses may be difficult. • Employee must retrace steps to leave work area. • Requires supervision/monitoring of the air supply line.

Adapted from: *Managing Hazardous Materials Incidents (Volume 1) – Emergency Medical Services: A Planning Guide for the Management of Contaminated Patients, Appendix B* (ATSDR, 2001 - www.atsdr.cdc.gov/mhmi/#bookmark05).

OSHA®
Occupational Safety and
Health Administration

Advantages and Disadvantages of Various
Respirator Facepiece Styles

Table J-3. Advantages and Disadvantages of Various Respirator Facepiece Styles

Facepiece style	Advantages	Disadvantages
Half facepiece	• Employee may wear any appropriate eyewear that does not interfere with the respirator seal.	• If there is a break in the seal between the mask and the face, contaminated air can enter. Fit testing must be performed prior to use and user seal checks must be done by the user every time the respirator is used. • Lower assigned protection factor than other facepieces. • Does not provide eye protection.
Full facepiece	• When used with a powered air-purifying respirator (PAPR), a tight fitting facepiece might allow an employee to pull filtered air into the facepiece if the battery fails. • Provides eye protection. • Better assigned protection factor, when fit is tested with quantitative methods.	• If there is a break in the seal between the mask and the face, contaminated air can enter. Fit testing must be performed prior to use and user seal checks must be done by the user every time the respirator is used. • Employees who wear glasses may require spectacle kits to be used inside the facepiece.
Loose fitting helmet/hood	• Provides eye protection from splashes. • Provides skin protection for the head and (certain models) neck. • Fit testing is not required. • Some employees find loose fitting respirators more comfortable than tight fitting models. • Can be worn by employees with facial hair and facial scars/deformities. • Employees may wear their own glasses under the helmet/hood.	• When used with a PAPR, provides little or no protection if the battery fails.
Adapted from *Personal Protective Equipment Guide for Military Medical Treatment Facility Personnel Handling Casualties from Weapons of Mass Destruction and Terrorism Events* (Technical Guide 275). U.S. Army Center for Health Promotion and Preventive Medicine (USACHPPM), August 2003.		

OSHA Assigned Protection Factors for Respiratory Protective Devices

Definition - Assigned protection factor (APF) (1910.134(b))

Assigned protection factor means the workplace level of respiratory protection that a respirator or class of respirators is expected to provide to employees when the employer implements a continuing, effective respiratory protection program as specified by this section.

Use of Assigned Protection Factors (APFs) (1910.134(d)(3)(i)(A))

Employers must use the assigned protection factors listed in [Table J-4] to select a respirator that meets or exceeds the required level of employee protection. When using a combination respirator (e.g., air-line respirators with an air-purifying filter), workers must ensure that the assigned protection factor is appropriate to the mode of operation in which the respirator is being used.

Table J-4. Assigned Protection Factors

Type of respirator [1,2,5]	Quarter mask	Half mask	Full facepiece	Helmet/ hood	Loose-fitting facepiece
1. Air-Purifying Respirator	5	10[3]	50	....	....
2. Powered Air-Purifying Respirator (PAPR)	....	50	1,000	25/1,000[4]	25
3. Supplied-Air Respirator (SAR) or Airline Respirator • Demand mode • Continuous flow mode • Pressure-demand or other positive-pressure mode		 10 50 50	 50 1,000 1,000	 .... 25/1,000[4]	 .... 25 ....
4. Self-Contained Breathing Apparatus (SCBA) • Demand mode • Pressure-demand or other positive-pressure mode (e.g., open/closed circuit)		 10	 50 10,000	 50 10,000	 ....

Notes:

[1] Employers may select respirators assigned for use in higher workplace concentrations of a hazardous substance for use at lower concentrations of that substance, or when required respirator use is independent of concentration.

[2] The assigned protection factors in this table are only effective when the employer implements a continuing, effective respirator program as required by this section (29 CFR 1910.134), including training, fit testing, maintenance, and use requirements.

[3] This APF category includes filtering facepieces, and half masks with elastomeric facepieces.

[4] The employer must have evidence provided by the respirator manufacturer that testing of these respirators demonstrates performance at a level of protection of 1,000 or greater to receive an APF of 1,000. This level of performance can best be demonstrated by performing a workplace protection factor (WPF) or simulated WPF (SWPF) study or equivalent testing. Absent such testing, all other PAPRs and SARs with helmets/hoods are to be treated as loose-fitting facepiece respirators, and receive an APF of 25.

[5] These APFs do not apply to respirators used solely for escape. For escape respirators used in association with specific substances covered by 29 CFR 1910 subpart Z, employers must refer to the appropriate substance-specific standards in that subpart. Escape respirators for other IDLH atmospheres are specified by 29 CFR 1910.134 (d)(2)(ii).

OSHA®
Occupational Safety and
Health Administration

Respirators for IDLH Atmospheres

Selected Excerpts from 29 CFR 1910.134 – OSHA's standard on Respiratory Protection

Hazard Evaluation (1910.134(d)(1)(iii))

The employer shall identify and evaluate the respiratory hazard(s) in the workplace; this evaluation shall include a reasonable estimate of employee exposures to respiratory hazard(s) and an identification of the contaminant's chemical state and physical form. Where the employer cannot identify or reasonably estimate the employee exposure, the employer shall consider the atmosphere to be IDLH.

The employer shall select respirators from a sufficient number of respirator models and sizes so that the respirator is acceptable to, and correctly fits, the user. (1910.134(d)(1)(iv))

Respirators for IDLH atmospheres (1910.134(d)(2))

The employer shall provide the following respirators for employee use in IDLH atmospheres:

A full facepiece pressure demand SCBA certified by NIOSH for a minimum service life of thirty minutes, or

A combination full facepiece pressure demand supplied-air respirator (SAR) with auxiliary self-contained air supply.

Respirators provided only for escape from IDLH atmospheres shall be NIOSH-certified for escape from the atmosphere in which they will be used.

All oxygen-deficient atmospheres shall be considered IDLH. Exception: If the employer demonstrates that, under all foreseeable conditions, the oxygen concentration can be maintained within the ranges specified [in Table II of the standard], then any atmosphere-supplying respirator may be used.

Respirators for Atmospheres that are Not IDLH

Respirators for atmospheres that are not IDLH (1910.134(d)(2)).

The employer shall provide a respirator that is adequate to protect the health of the employee and ensure compliance with all other OSHA statutory and regulatory requirements, under routine and reasonably foreseeable emergency situations.

Choosing APR Cartridges that Offer Protection Against a Wide Range of Contaminants

The combination of high efficiency (P-100) particulate filters plus organic vapor (OV) cartridges in what has come to be known as "stacked cartridges" will protect against many of the airborne hazards that EMTs might encounter (e.g., toxic dusts, biological agents, radioactive particulates, organophosphates and other pesticides, and solvents).[33] Acid gas and amine cartridges add an additional level of protection from gases which have been implicated in at least one case of healthcare worker injury.[34]

---

[33] For PAPRs the equivalent to a P-100 filter is the high efficiency (HE) filter.

[34] Despite the number of carbon monoxide victims treated at hospitals, it is not anticipated that EMS responders would benefit from specialty cartridges that remove carbon monoxide from air. There are no reported cases of healthcare workers being injured through secondary contamination from victims of carbon monoxide poisoning (Horton et al., 2003; Hick et al., 2003; Walter et al., 2003). If the source of carbon monoxide is producing an ongoing release, appropriately trained responders equipped with SCBA will need to control the release and evacuate victims.

Appendix K

Heat Stress and Strain

EMS responders must work in a wide variety of hot or hot and humid environments. Comfort is not the only issue in working in such environments. Workers who are suddenly exposed to working in a hot environment face additional and generally avoidable hazards to their safety and health. Chemical protective clothing can add an extra burden by reducing air circulation on the skin and limiting the body's natural ability to cool itself as sweat evaporates. Extended use of respiratory protection can also hinder a worker's ability to replenish fluids by drinking, putting the worker at greater risk. The employer should provide detailed instructions on preventive measures and adequate protection necessary to prevent heat stress. Detailed guidance on preventive measures can be found in the following documents.

NIOSH Publication No. 86-112 – *Working in Hot Environments* provides basic general information for employers and employees on thermal stress from working in hot environments. Access this publication at www.cdc.gov/niosh/hotenvt.html# protective

The problems of thermal stress and chemical protective clothing are outlined in paragraph X of OSHA's Technical Manual, Section VII, Chapter 1 – *Chemical Protective Clothing* www.osha.gov/dts/osta/otm/otm_viii/otm_viii_1.html

Cold Stress and Hypothermia

Dust EMS responders who assist patients during incidents involving cold weather may be subject to cold exposure, which can affect performance and ultimately lead to hyperthermia. Wet conditions (including sweat) and wind can exacerbate the situation. Decontamination procedures often mean greater exposure to water and removal of clothes resulting in greater exposure to cold and wind. Effective alternate decontamination methods should be considered in extremely cold climates.

The U.S. Army Technical Bulletin TB-MED 508 – *Prevention and Management of Cold-weather Injuries* offers details on cold stress management. Section 3-2 provides guidance on avoiding hypothermia, while Section 3-6 offers suggestions for PPE use and decontamination in very cold weather. Although intended for military troops, the advice (e.g., straps on the respirator mask must not be too tight, as this will reduce blood flow to the skin of the face and can cause frostbite) applies to any worker wearing protective gear at extremely low temperatures. www.usariem.army.mil/ download/tbmed508.pdf

Appendix L

Decontamination foams have been the subject of research by Sandia National Laboratories. These foams are effective for use on equipment against certain biological and chemical contaminants. These products have been licensed for commercial production (EnviroFoam, 2008; Modec, 2008). The foams have not been approved for use on human skin.

For certain weapons of chemical, biological, radiological, nuclear, or explosive (CBRNE) contaminants (nerve and blister agents, specifically), Reactive Skin Decontamination Lotion (RSDL) offers some benefit but has some inherent risk. The FDA has approved this lotion for use on human skin. According to the product distributor, the U.S. military is conducting efficacy testing and recently began permitting local police, fire departments, emergency medical teams, and the other organizations to use the lotion (E-Z-EM, 2006).

Another product under development by the military, Skin Exposure Reduction Paste Against Chemical Warfare Agents (SERPACWA), is also intended for use on human skin (Ellen, 2003). This product functions as a barrier cream when applied before any opportunity for exposure occurs. The cream is intended to protect military personnel from adverse effects if a small amount of contaminant penetrates through "hastily donned full-body protective gear." It is hoped that a related product (active topical skin protectant), also under development, will offer greater protection. Neither of these products is FDA approved.

Appendix M

Examples of PPE Donning and
Doffing Sequences

PPE Donning Sequence

(NOTE: The following sequence outlines the order in which some EMS personnel find it efficient to put on their specific PPE. This sequence was developed for personnel who would wear a hooded PAPR respirator, chemical protective suit, gloves and boots. The sequence may be adapted for other types of respirators and protective equipment. The list is not intended to provide detailed step-by-step instructions for putting on the PPE.)

1. Test PAPR flow rate to be sure it meets rate specified by the manufacturer.
2. Remove jewelry & clothing.
3. Put on inner nitrile gloves.
4. In COLD WEATHER: Put on inner suit. Tape gloves at wrist & zipper at neck.
5. In WARM WEATHER: Put on scrubs.
6. Put on outer chemical protective suit to waist. Put on boots & outer chemical protective gloves.
7. Connect PAPR to hood with hose; turn airflow on. Put on butyl hood (position the inside shroud between suits). Pull chemical protective suit up and on.
8. Ensure zipper is covered & secured, put tape on top.
9. Belt PAPR to waist.
10. Put outer butyl hood shroud over suit.
11. Stretch arms, pull suit sleeves OVER gloves, tape in place.
12. Pull suit cuff over boot top, tape in place.
13. Place a piece of tape on the hood exterior and label with the employee's name & time that employee is entering the warm zone.

PPE Decontamination & Doffing Sequence

(NOTE: The following sequence outlines the order in which some EMS personnel find it effective to decontaminate themselves and their PPE as one procedure, to minimize the chance of contaminating their skin while removing their PPE. This sequence was developed for personnel who would wear a hooded PAPR respirator, chemical protective suit, gloves and boots. The sequence may be adapted for other types of respirators and protective equipment. The list is not intended to provide detailed step-by-step instructions.)

1. Wash hands thoroughly.
2. Still wearing PPE, wash self, starting at the top of the head and working down to the bottom of the boots. Have a partner wash your back.
3. Untape boots and gloves, but do not remove them.
4. Unlock PAPR and place it on chair/gurney/floor, etc.
5. Remove the outer suit—roll the suit away from you, inside out (with help from a partner).
6. Remove outer gloves along with the outer suit.
7. Remove PAPR hood, place in waste.
8. Step out of boots and suit into final rinse area (keep inner gloves and clothing on). Wash and rinse thoroughly (with partner's help).
9. In COLD WEATHER: Remove (inner) suit, place in waste.
10. Remove nitrile gloves: first pinch one glove and roll it down partially, then place thumb in other glove & remove both gloves simultaneously.
11. Wash again, removing inner clothing, then step out of decontamination shower and into towels/blankets.

Source: Adapted from *Managing Hazardous Materials Incidents* (Volume II). *Hospital Emergency Departments: A Planning Guide for the Management of Contaminated Patients.* U.S. Department of Health and Human Services. Public Health Service. Agency for Toxic Substances and Disease Registry (Revised 2000). www.atsdr.cdc.gov

Occupational Safety and
Health Administration

Appendix N

This appendix, taken from Appendix B of OSHA's HAZWOPER standard (29 CFR 1910.120) and adapted with additional information from Appendix C of ATSDR (2001), sets forth information about personal protective equipment (PPE) protection levels that may be used to assist employers in complying with the PPE requirements of the HAZWOPER standard.

As required by the HAZWOPER standard, PPE must be selected which will protect employees from the specific hazards which they are likely to encounter during their work.

Selection of the appropriate PPE is a complex process which should take into consideration a variety of factors. Key factors involved in this process are identification of the hazards, or suspected hazards; the routes by which employees could be exposed to the potential hazard (inhalation, skin absorption, ingestion, and eye or skin contact); and the performance of the PPE materials (and seams) in providing a barrier to these hazards. The amount of protection provided by PPE is material- and hazard-specific. That is, protective equipment materials will protect well against some hazardous substances and poorly, or not at all, against others. In many instances, protective equipment materials cannot be found which will provide continuous protection from the particular hazardous substance. In these cases, the PPE must be changed or work must stop before breakthrough time is reached (55 FR 14074, Apr. 13, 1990).

Other factors in this selection process to be considered are matching the PPE to the employee's work requirements and task-specific conditions. The durability of PPE materials, such as tear strength and seam strength, should be considered in relation to the employee's tasks. The effects of PPE in relation to heat stress and task duration are a factor in selecting and using PPE. In some cases layers of PPE may be necessary to provide sufficient protection, or to protect expensive PPE inner garments, suits, or equipment.

The more that is known about the hazards at the site, the easier the job of PPE selection becomes. As more information about the hazards and conditions at the site becomes available, the site supervisor can make decisions to upgrade or downgrade the level of PPE to match the tasks at hand.

The following are guidelines which an employer can use to begin the selection of the appropriate PPE. As noted above, the site information may suggest the use of combinations of PPE selected from the different protection levels (i.e., A, B, C, or D) as being more suitable to the hazards of the work. It should be cautioned that the listing below does not fully address the performance of the specific PPE material in relation to the specific hazards at the job site, and that PPE selection, evaluation and reselection is an ongoing process as sufficient information about the hazards and PPE performance is obtained.

Personal protective equipment is divided into four categories based on the degree of protection afforded. Table N-1 presents the recommended equipment, suggestions for when it should be used, and limiting criteria associated with this level of PPE.

Table N-1. PPE Levels of Protection

Level of Protection	Equipment	Should be Used When	Limiting Criteria
Level A Offers the highest available level of respiratory, skin, and eye protection.	• Positive pressure, full facepiece self-contained breathing apparatus (SCBA), or positive pressure supplied air respirator with escape SCBA, approved by the National Institute for Occupational Safety and Health (NIOSH). • Totally-encapsulating chemical-protective suit. • Coveralls.* • Long underwear.* • Gloves, outer, chemical-resistant. • Gloves, inner, chemical-resistant. • Boots, chemical-resistant, steel toe and shank. • Hard hat (under suit).* • Disposable protective suit, gloves and boots (depending on suit construction, may be worn over totally-encapsulating suit).	• The hazardous substance has been identified and requires the highest level of protection for skin, eyes, and the respiratory system based on either the measured (or potential for) high concentration of atmospheric vapors, gases, or particulates; or the site operations and work functions involve a high potential for splash, immersion, or exposure to unexpected vapors, gases, or particulates of materials that are harmful to skin or capable of being absorbed through the skin. • Substances with a high degree of hazard to the skin are known or suspected to be present, and skin contact is possible, or • Operations must be conducted in confined, poorly ventilated areas, and the absence of conditions requiring Level A have not yet been determined.	Fully encapsulated suit; material must be compatible with the substances involved.

Level of Protection	Equipment	Should be Used When	Limiting Criteria
Level B Offers the same level of respiratory protection, but less skin protection than Level A. It is the minimum level recommended for initial site entries until the hazards have been further identified.	• Positive pressure, full-facepiece self-contained breathing apparatus (SCBA), or positive pressure supplied air respirator with escape SCBA (NIOSH approved). • Hooded chemical-resistant clothing (overalls and long-sleeved jacket; coveralls; one or two-piece chemical-splash suit; disposable chemical-resistant overalls). • Coveralls.* • Gloves, outer, chemical-resistant. • Gloves, inner, chemical-resistant. • Boots, outer, chemical-resistant steel toe and shank. • Boot-covers, outer, chemical-resistant (disposable).* • Hard hat.* • Face shield.*	• The type and atmospheric concentration of substances have been identified and require a high level of respiratory protection, but less skin protection. • The atmosphere contains less than 19.5 percent oxygen; or • The presence of incompletely identified vapors or gases is indicated by a direct-reading organic vapor detection instrument, but vapors and gases are not suspected of containing high levels of chemicals harmful to skin or capable of being absorbed through the skin. • Note: This involves atmospheres with IDLH concentrations of specific substances that present severe inhalation hazards and that do not represent a severe skin hazard; or that do not meet the criteria for use of air-purifying respirators.	Use only when the vapor or gases present are not suspected of containing high concentrations of chemicals that are harmful to skin or capable of being absorbed through intact skin. Use only when it is highly unlikely that the work being done will generate either high concentrations of vapors, gases, or particulates or splashes of material that will affect exposed skin.

Level of Protection	Equipment	Should be Used When	Limiting Criteria
Level C The level of air purifying respiratory protection depends on the type of facepiece and fit testing performed. Offers limited skin protection.	• Full-face or half-mask, air purifying respirators (NIOSH approved). • Hooded chemical-resistant clothing (overalls; two-piece chemical-splash suit; disposable chemical-resistant overalls). • Coveralls.* • Gloves, outer, chemical-resistant. • Gloves, inner, chemical-resistant. • Boots (outer), chemical-resistant steel toe and shank.* • Boot-covers, outer, chemical-resistant (disposable).* • Hard hat.* • Escape mask.* • Face shield.*	• The atmospheric contaminants, liquid splashes, or other direct contact will not adversely affect or be absorbed through any exposed skin; • The types of air contaminants have been identified, concentrations measured, and an air-purifying respirator is available that can remove the contaminants; and • All criteria for the use of air-purifying respirators are met.	This level should not be worn in the hot zone. The atmosphere must contain at least 19.5 percent oxygen.
Level D No respiratory protection; minimal skin protection.	• Coveralls. • Gloves.* • Boots/shoes, chemical-resistant steel toe and shank. • Boots, outer, chemical-resistant (disposable).* • Safety glasses or chemical splash goggles.* • Hard hat.* • Escape mask.* • Face shield.*	• The atmosphere contains no known hazard; and • Work functions preclude splashes, immersion, or the potential for unexpected inhalation of or contact with hazardous levels of any chemicals.	This level should not be worn in the hot zone. The atmosphere must contain at least 19.5 percent oxygen.

NOTES:
*=Optional, as applicable.

As stated before, combinations of personal protective equipment other than those described for Levels A, B, C, and D protection may be more appropriate and may be used to provide the proper level of protection.
Source: 29 CFR 1910.120, Appendix B – General description and discussion of the levels of protection and protective gear.

Appendix O

Background/Overview

Employers' decisions regarding worker protection must begin with an evaluation of the hazards to which workers might be exposed. A review of the literature shows that EMS responders are subject to many of the same occupational safety and health hazards as are workers in other transportation, medical, and public service occupations. EMS responders are subject to hazardous substance exposures as well as numerous other hazards, including back injuries, automobile crashes, assault, stress, bloodborne pathogens, and injuries to the extremities, eyes, and ears.

Review of the Literature on Risks to EMS Responders

Experience of EMS Responders Exposed to Hazardous Substances

EMS responders routinely respond to sites where hazardous substance releases have occurred. The responders can become exposed to hazardous substances when they provide medical treatment at these sites or at locations where contaminated persons, equipment, or vehicles have been moved after the release. Although most studies of hazardous substance exposure only looked at the broader group of emergency service providers (including various combinations of firefighters, police, EMTs, HAZMAT teams, and in some cases emergency room personnel), several reports provided detailed information specific to EMS responders.[35] OSHA has summarized those reports in the following section.

EMTs at the Tokyo Subway Sarin Gas Attacks

The experience of EMTs was specifically documented for the Tokyo subway sarin gas attacks of 1995. In that disaster, officials dispatched 1,364 EMTs and 131 ambulances (plus some minivans) to 15 affected subway stations, from which they transported 688 of the 4,000 victims who eventually were seen at area hospitals. A review of incident records indicated that 135 (9.9%) of the EMTs showed acute symptoms and received medical treatment at hospitals.[36] The authors did not indicate whether EMTs

entered the contaminated subway areas, but indicated that they did assist contaminated victims. Most of the affected EMTs "started having symptoms during transportation, and it is suspected that they were exposed in ambulances to the vaporized sarin from victims' clothes." (Okumura et al., 1998). The EMTs "wore standard work clothing without respiratory protection" and "ventilation in ambulances and minivans at first was poor" because windows were closed, although these were later opened to improve the ventilation in transport vehicles.[37]

Okumura et al. (1998) note that it is important to consider several additional factors when evaluating the experience of EMTs during this disaster, including the lack of proper patient decontamination, the duties performed by EMTs in Japan, and the ratio of victims that arrived at the hospital via ambulance compared to other forms of transportation. These additional factors are described in more detail here:

- Lack of decontamination: Little or no effort was made to decontaminate victims before transporting them (Okumura et al., 1998). If performed, these types of decontamination activities might have significantly reduced victim exposure levels, particularly because many victims experienced continued exposure while they waited in crowded, enclosed rooms before being treated at hospitals. While earlier efforts to decontaminate the victims would likely have reduced EMT exposures during victim transport, the act of decontamination might have contributed to the exposure of EMTs who assisted victims with washing and undressing. Sarin off-gassing from abandoned contaminated clothing could also have continued to present a source of exposure to EMTs in the area. EMTs would have required additional precautions to operate safely.

- EMT duties: Okumura et al. (2004) point out that "Under Japanese law, only physicians are allowed to perform endotracheal intubation and administer medications to victims of a chemical attack at the site of the incident." In Japan, emergency response physicians can be dispatched for this purpose (in contrast, EMS personnel in the U.S. are often authorized to perform intubation). Hick et al. (2003) also reviewed the literature describing this incident and noted that the healthcare employees most affected were several

---

[35] Historically, "general-population sources [of injury and illness data] contain information on police and firefighters, but EMS personnel are not typically broken out." (Houser et al., 2004).

[36] The authors did not elaborate on the symptoms, but imply that the acute symptoms were considered possible effects of sarin exposure.

---

[37] An important consideration for those planning EMS responder protection is that "even in the absence of risk, the *perceived* risk without PPE can lead to symptoms and compromise workflow." Hick (2007).

physicians who spent up to 40 minutes attempting to resuscitate the initial victims of the incident. As might be expected, the medical personnel most affected provided treatment involving extended close contact with the most critically ill victims – who were also likely to have been the most highly exposed and perhaps the most highly contaminated.

- Victim transportation to the hospital: Records from one Tokyo hospital indicate that, while the greatest number of victims arrived by foot, the percentage who arrived by taxi (24 percent of all victims arriving at that hospital) was more than three times the number transported by ambulance (7 percent). Another 13 percent arrived by private vehicles (Okumura et al., 1998). Although it might be assumed that the most severely exposed and affected victims were transported by ambulance, two of the three reported cardiac arrest cases were transported by private vehicles that happened to be passing the subway station shortly after the incident (Okumura et al., 1998). Although victims were triaged at the subway stations, some victims worsened during transport, suggesting greater or continuing exposures. This suggests that if more victims had been transported by ambulance, more EMTs might have experienced the effects of exposure. A follow-up evaluation of rescue team members and police officers, made 2 to 3 years after they had been exposed to sarin in the Tokyo incident, suggested a decline in memory function independent of traumatic stress symptoms. The authors were not able to determine whether the effect was due to direct neurotoxicity of sarin (Nishiwaki et al., 2001).

Hazardous Substances Emergency Events Surveillance (HSEES) Data for EMS Responders

Horton et al. (2003 and 2008) and ATSDR (2004 and 2007) reported on the experience of EMTs responding to events recorded in the Hazardous Substances Emergency Events Surveillance (HSEES) system.[38] For the purposes of this database, a hazardous substance was any substance (i.e., chemical, biological, or radiological) that could reasonably be expected to cause an adverse health effect. Events involving only petroleum are excluded by HSEES. Hazardous substance emergency events were defined as "actual, uncontrolled, or illegal releases of a hazardous substance(s) that had to be removed, cleaned up, or neutralized according to federal, state, or local law." Victims of such events were defined as "persons sustaining at least one injury or symptom (i.e., respiratory irritation) or death as a result of the event."

The HSEES data for seven years from 1995 through 2001 show that EMTs constituted one-half of one percent (0.5 percent) of all reported victims of hazardous substance emergency events (13,173 total victims from more than 44,000 events) recorded during this period. Altogether, 72 EMT injuries were reported.[39] The 13,173 total victims also included 190 volunteer firefighters, 273 career firefighters, 437 police officers, and 32 hospital personnel, indicating that first responders (of all types) accounted for a notable number victims injured during reported events of this period (Horton et al., 2003).

A subsequent report reviewed the frequency with which medical treatment and decontamination were provided during HSEES events. These HSEES data indicate that medical treatment (first aid) was provided (presumably by EMS responders in most cases) for 262 injuries sustained by individuals at hazardous substance release sites in the year 2004 (ATSDR, 2004). Figure O-1, reprinted from ATSDR (2004), contrasts this value to the 1,039 hazardous substance release site injuries treated in hospitals. These figures suggest that EMS responders are being called to some scenes to treat patients, but that the vast majority of victims injured in hazardous substance release events are being transported or otherwise finding their way to hospitals for treatment (in some cases, possibly in addition to treatment at the scene).

Decontamination is performed infrequently, but is somewhat more likely to occur at the scene of the release than at medical facilities. "Of the 1,766 (96.0%) victims [in 2004 for whom decontamination status was reported to HSEES], 1,483 (84.0%) were not decontaminated, 157 (8.9%) were decontaminated at the scenes, 101 (5.7%) were decontaminated at medical facilities, and 25 (1.4%) were decontaminated at both the scenes and medical facilities." (ATSDR, 2004).

Victims who were decontaminated in 2004 were not necessarily injured. "For events in which uninjured persons were decontaminated, the median number of uninjured decontaminated individuals

---

[38] The HSEES system data were collected by the Agency for Toxic Substances and Disease Registry (ATSDR). The 16 reporting states included (grouped by geographical area): Alabama, Mississippi, Texas, Iowa, Missouri, Minnesota, Wisconsin, New York, New Jersey, Rhode Island, New Hampshire, North Carolina, Colorado, Oregon, Washington, and Utah (Horton et al., 2003; Berkowitz et al., 2004). Two additional states, Florida and Michigan, began reporting in 2006 (Horton et al., 2008). Not all states participated for the full period.

[39] Horton et al. (2003) reported that 3,453 of these approximately 44,000 events involved injured victims; however, the total number of EMTs responding to these events is not known.

OSHA®
Occupational Safety and
Health Administration

was 3 persons per event (range: 1–100 persons). Decontamination was done at the scene for 144 uninjured employees, 451 uninjured responders, 140 uninjured members of the general public, and 72 uninjured students." Decontamination was done at medical facilities for 4 uninjured employees, 3 uninjured responders, and 20 uninjured members of the general public (ATSDR 2004). Information is not available on the class of responders performing decontamination at the scene.

An evaluation of more recent HSEES data looked specifically at secondary contamination of medical personnel, equipment, and facilities that resulted from hazardous materials events during the four years from the beginning of 2003 through 2006 (Horton et al., 2008). The authors evaluated secondary exposure during three phases of the events: The Hazmat phase (at the site of the hazardous substance release), the transport phase (during transit to a medical treatment facility), and the hospital phase. EMTs are likely to have been the personnel primarily involved in providing medical treatment during the Hazmat and transport phases.

During the four-year period, 33,157 events were reported, 15 (0.05 percent) of which resulted in secondary contamination of 17 medical personnel (12 EMTs and five hospital employees) and 15 ambulances. Nearly three-quarters of these 15 events occurred at fixed facilities, while approximately one-quarter were transportation-related incidents. The authors reported that during the Hazmat phase of these events, 47 non-medical personnel were also injured (primarily respiratory irritation) and 42 people were decontaminated at the scene of release.

The data suggest that EMS responder injuries were more likely to occur when the substance release involved a vapor or aerosol compared to spilled liquids or solids. Causal information was only available for 14 of the 15 events and indicated an equal number of the events (7 events) were caused by accidents due to human error as were caused by intentional or illegal acts (also 7 events). Three of the events were associated with clandestine methamphetamine labs (Horton et al., 2008).

During the transportation phase, at least one ambulance was contaminated in each of the 13 events during which patients were transported by ambulance. Respiratory irritation was the most frequent injury among the 12 reported EMT injuries due to secondary contamination during the transport phase. Two of the 12 EMTs (17 percent) wore exam gloves (not chemical-resistant), while the other 10 EMTs were wearing no PPE when they were injured. None of the EMTs had received HAZWOPER training (Horton et al., 2008).

The HSEES data from an overlapping period, including the years 2002 through 2006, were reviewed in a separate analysis that specifically assessed EMT/EMS involvement in hazardous substance release events (ATSDR, 2007). In those five years, 54,729 incidents were reported with EMTs responding to 4,138 (8 percent). Of 11,293 total injuries reported during this period, 38 (0.3 percent) were associated with EMT/EMS who responded and then were injured at the scene of the hazardous substance release. The 38 EMT/EMS injuries averaged over the 4,138 scenes to which EMT/EMS responded, suggest that on average an EMS responder experiences injury at a rate of slightly less than 1 injury per 100 HSEES events to which EMTs responded (0.9 percent). The data also show that during this same period, 894 victims (9 percent) were decontaminated at the scene.

Figures O-2 through O-4 present additional information on the HSEES events at which EMT/EMS injuries occurred. Figure O-2 illustrates that these EMS responder injuries were more often associated with an aerosol or vapor release (two-thirds of the injuries), compared to a solid or liquid spill (ATSDR, 2007). Figure O-3 compares the relative frequency with which specific symptoms were reported in EMT/EMS personnel injured at the scene. Note that multiple injuries reported for the same victim are recorded individually in HSEES; as a result, the total number of reported injuries is greater than the number of injured EMT/EMS personnel. Respiratory irritation accounted for 39 percent of the EMT/EMS injuries and was reported nearly twice as often as the next most frequent symptom, dizziness/central nervous system (CNS) effects (17 percent). A wide variety of chemical substances were released at sites where EMT/EMT injuries occurred, as indicated by Figure O-4 (ATSDR, 2007).

Figure O-2. Release Type for Incidents at Which EMS Responders Were Injured (HSEES 2002-2007)

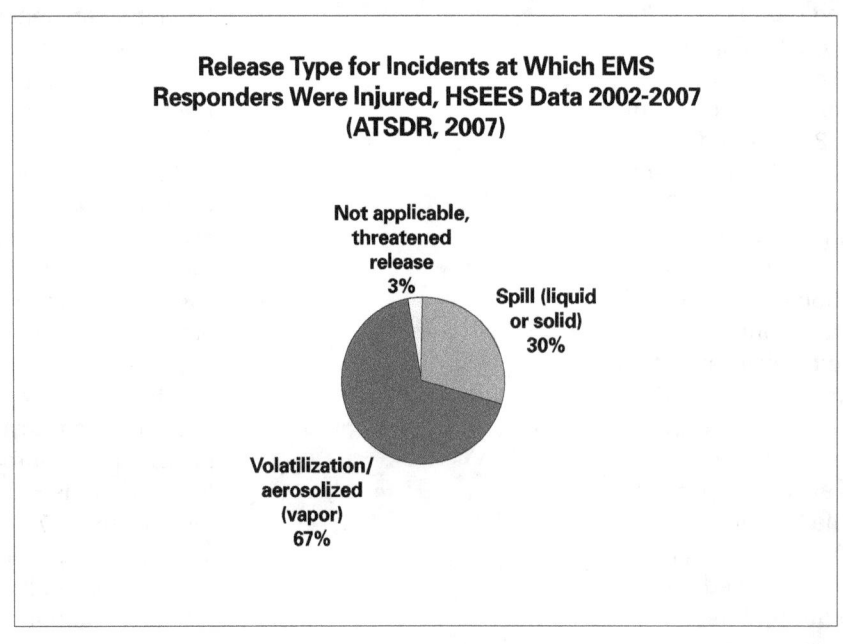

OSHA®
Occupational Safety and
Health Administration

Figure O-3. Frequency of Specific Symptoms Among EMT/EMS Injured at Scenes with Hazardous Substance Release (HSEES 2002-2006)

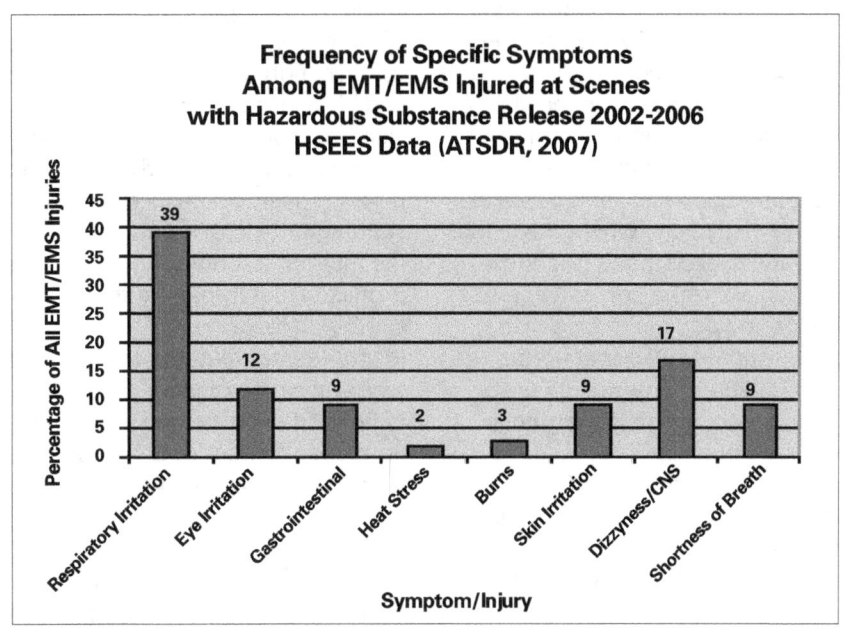

Figure O-4. Chemical Categories Associated with Hazardous Substance Release – Scenes at Which EMT/EMS Were Injured (HSEES 2002-2006)

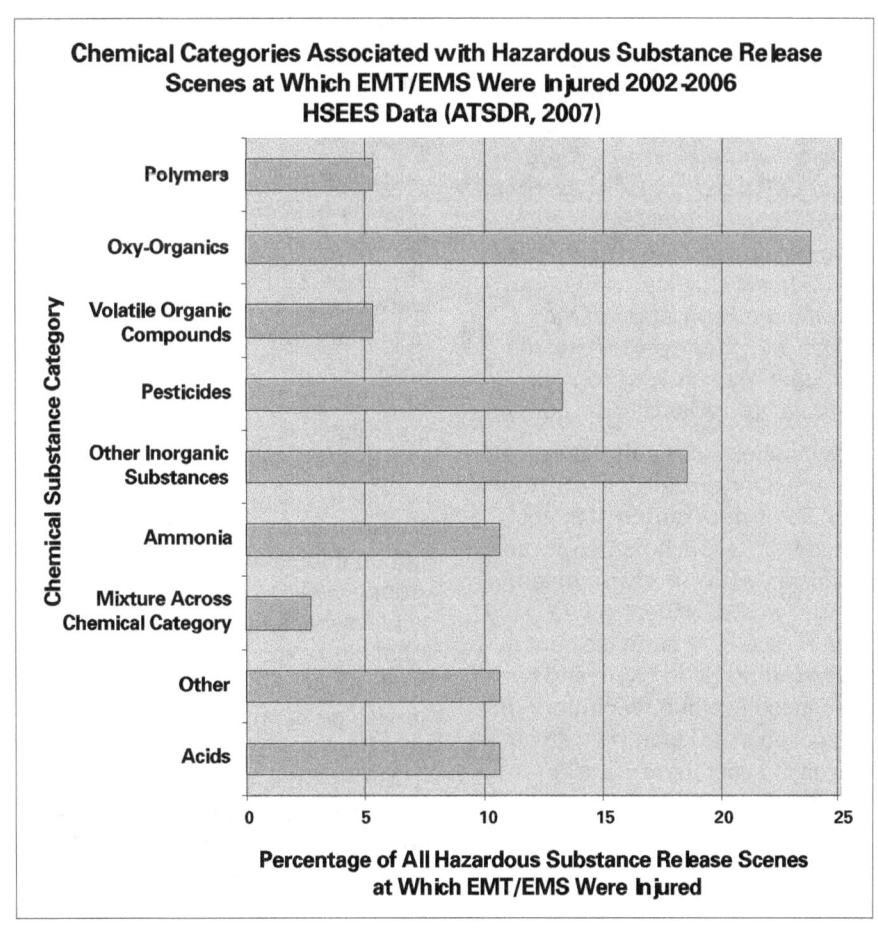

The published literature contains several other reports of hazardous substance effects on EMS personnel responding to clandestine drug laboratories, acts of terrorism, and transportation incidents in the U.S.

Response to clandestine methamphetamine laboratories presents an increasing source of hazardous substance exposure, injuries, and illnesses to EMS responders in jurisdictions where these labs are prevalent. "Substances used in the methamphetamine laboratories are often corrosive, explosive, flammable, and toxic and can cause fires, explosions, and other uncontrolled reactions." (MMWR, November 17, 2000). The results are devastating to laboratory occupants, emergency responders, and the local public.

Berkowitz et al. (2004) analyzed HSEES data between 1993 and 2000 and found that the nine reports of EMS responders injured during hazardous substance release events all occurred in non-rural areas. This trend is in contrast to the finding that emergency responders in general (and volunteer firefighters in particular) were three times more likely to be injured in rural/agricultural areas than in other areas. The report continues:

> "Of note was the large proportion of victims who were responders, mainly police officers and EMTs, in the events involving drug laboratories. More than half of these events involved fire and/or explosion, and almost all injured police officers and EMTs did not wear personal protective clothes. These circumstances indicate that responders typically are very vulnerable to hazardous exposures. They often enter the event area with little knowledge of the chemicals involved, and they do not have the proper protection that may prevent contact with these chemicals." (Berkowitz et al., 2004)

Although injuries resulted from only 7.2 percent of all the hazardous substance incidents reported by five states to the HSEES system during 1996 to 1999, injuries resulted from a much higher portion (52.7 percent) of incidents when methamphetamine processing was a factor at the incident scene (MMWR, November 17, 2000).[40] In one incident in April 1996, three Washington State EMTs and two police officers experienced eye and respiratory irritation after being exposed in an apartment to emissions from a fire involving acetone, hydrochloric acid, and sodium hydroxide in an illicit metham-

phetamine lab. Overall, symptoms reported by EMS responders across all five states included eight cases of respiratory tract irritation (47.1 percent of EMS responders reported symptoms), four cases of eye irritation (23.5 percent), two cases of nausea and vomiting (11.8 percent), and one report each of skin irritation, headache, and shortness of breath (each 5.9 percent). "EMTs sustained most injuries through onsite exposure or direct contact with the clothing or skin of contaminated persons.... None of the injured first responders was wearing personal protective equipment at the time of injury." (MMWR, November 17, 2000). The associated MMWR editorial noted that "standard uniforms worn by police officers, EMTs, and hospital personnel provided little or no chemical/respiratory protection." See Appendix G for additional discussion of response to clandestine methamphetamine laboratories.

EMS personnel who responded to the World Trade Center rescue effort in 2001 visited healthcare facilities 183 times. The most common complaints were musculoskeletal injuries (38 cases), headache (21 cases), respiratory effects other than acute infection (18 cases), eye irritation or injury (17 cases), and skin problems (11 cases) (Berrios-Torres et al., 2003). Most of the affected EMS responders were treated and released; there were no fatalities among this group and only one EMS responder was admitted to a hospital. The authors could not determine incident rates for these injuries and illnesses because the total number of individuals working in the capacity of EMS responder during the response was not recorded. This study evaluated injuries and illnesses for which various groups of first responders were treated and results do not reflect the number of firefighters who died in the World Trade Center disaster.

Other studies shed light on exposure patterns of emergency response personnel in general (not specific to EMS responders). One review of injuries caused by hazardous materials accidents in Massachusetts between 1990 and 1996 found that "when injuries did occur, they were more frequently among civilians (25 percent of the incidents) than public service personnel (7 percent of the incidents). Inhalation exposure was more common [among the public] than dermal exposure, while injury to public service personnel involved only minor musculoskeletal injuries." (Kales et al., 1997).

Six first responders were among 44 people injured in Texas when a tanker car was punctured during a train derailment in 2004. "At least 60,000 pounds of chlorine (as released gas) reacted with sodium hydroxide to form sodium hypochlorite,

---

[40] The five states were Iowa, Minnesota, Missouri, Oregon, and Washington.

killing two people. [EMS] personnel were among the first responders at the scene." (MMWR, 2005). Eighty first responders were decontaminated after responding to the event.

Compared to the amount of information available for firefighters and police, relatively few reports provide injury and illness statistics specifically for EMS responders. The more general emergency responder information, however, has some inferential value. A Rand report (Houser et al., 2004) rates the applicability of available emergency services casualty data (for firefighters, police, etc.) to EMS responders.[41] The report classifies the relevance of general emergency services data to the experience of EMS responders as "medium" for fatal and non-fatal injury and illness. On the other hand, for HAZMAT incidents, the applicability of general emergency services data to the experience of EMS responders is rated as "high," suggesting that the author considered many of the determinants of hazardous materials exposure similar for responders in various specialties (e.g., fire, HAZMAT, medical, and police).

Risk to EMS Responders of Injury and Illness from Causes Other than Hazardous Substance Exposure

As shown in the previous section, hazardous substance exposure is a real concern for EMS responders, but is far from the only concern. For comparison, this section describes other causes of injury and illnesses in EMS responders (i.e., not related to hazardous substances).

Injury and illness statistics support the need for safer work practices. In a survey of registered EMTs in New England, Schwartz et al. (1993) described self-reported injury rates (for back, stress, assault, hearing loss, eye injury, ambulance collision, etc.).[42]

---

[41] For example, the authors analyzed how closely study findings based on data covering the combined experience of firefighters, police, and other types of emergency responders (defined as "general emergency services data") would track the actual experience of EMS responders. The authors rated EMS personnel's risk of fatal injury or illness (e.g., due to collapse of a burning structure or gunfire) as lower than that of firefighters and police, while the hazardous materials exposure of EMS personnel was rated as more similar (but not necessarily identical) to that of firefighters and police.

[42] Questionnaires were mailed to a random sample (2 percent) of all registered EMTs in Vermont, New Hampshire, Rhode Island, Maine, Connecticut, and Massachusetts. Fifty-six percent of the 786 surveys were successfully returned. The average responder was 35 years old with 8 years on the job (ranging from less than 1 year to 36 years of EMT experience) (Schwartz et al., 1993). Note that the low return rate is a possible source of bias in the study, which could have lead to an over-representation of injury rates as EMTs who had been injured might be more likely to return the survey.

The average prevalence rates, standardized to the number of occurrences per 100 full-time equivalent (FTE) EMTs per year, were highest for stress that interfered with the job (prevalence rate of 27.1), back injury (25.4), and injuries to extremities (23.7). Over half the back injuries resulted in lost workdays, the average being 25 days, and the range from 2 to 180 days. EMTs reported being assaulted at a rate of 20.3 occurrences per 100 FTE EMTs/year and being involved in an ambulance collision at a prevalence rate of 9.9 occurrences per 100 FTE EMTs/year. Eye injury (due to foreign objects or chemicals) and hearing loss were reported less frequently, with prevalence rates of 3.4 and 6.0, respectively; however, even these values potentially represent a large number of affected individuals, considering that there were over 38,000 registered EMTs at the time that this survey was conducted.[43]

Gershon et al. (1995) also investigated accidents and injuries among EMS responders in the early 1990s. In this case, the research evaluated medical charts for EMS responders employed by a county fire department, which conducted approximately 32,000 emergency responses in 1992. EMS employees filed 226 injury reports: 23 percent related to sprains, 20 percent to strains, and 15 percent in response to exposure to body fluids. The back (20 percent) and respiratory tract (15 percent) were the sites most frequently injured. "Most incidents were caused by stretcher mishaps, especially during transport of heavy patients."

In a more recent retrospective review, Maguire et al. (2005) studied on-duty injury reports recorded between 1998 and 2002 for two EMS agencies that were the sole 9-1-1 EMS providers in large urban areas (civilian, non-firefighting). Agency employees logged over 2.8 million hours and experienced 489 reported injuries over the period studied (227 of these involved lost work time). The overall injury rate was 34.6 per 100 FTEs/year, with sprains, strains, and tears the most frequent category of injury, and the back the most frequently injured site. The authors conclude, "Our findings have shown that the rate of injuries among EMS workers was higher than the rate for any private industry published by the [Department of Labor] in 2000."

Other investigators also found that transportation-related crashes and assaults contributed substantially to EMS responder injury rates, with EMS responders accounting for 33 percent of fatalities

---

[43] The authors were not able to determine the proportion of all registered EMTs that were full-time, part-time, or not actively working in the field. The survey respondents, however, worked an average of 33 hours per week.

associated with ambulance occupants in crashes. The authors cited inconsistent seatbelt/restraint use as a weak point in EMS responder vehicular safety (MMWR, February 28, 2003). Kahn et al. (2001) reviewed fatal ambulance crash records from 1987 to 1997, confirming that the most serious or fatal injuries occurred in the rear (compared to the front driver compartment) and were associated with improperly restrained occupants. The authors also found that 41 percent of ambulance drivers had poor driving records and 16 percent had been cited for traffic violations.

EMS responders also experience elevated occupational mortality and ground transportation-related fatalities that are a significant factor in the estimated fatality rate for EMS personnel. For this group, the fatality rate from all causes was 12.7 deaths per 100,000, more than twice the national average of 5.0 deaths per 100,000 for the same period (Maguire et al., 2002; MMWR, February 28, 2003). The authors reviewed three independent fatality databases from approximately 1992 to 1997 and estimated there were 114 EMS employee fatalities during those 6 years, including at least 67 ground transportation-related fatalities, 19 air ambulance crash fatalities, 13 deaths resulting from cardiovascular incidents, 10 homicides, and 5 deaths due to other causes (Maguire et al., 2002). Citing more recent data from the National EMS Memorial Service, Houser et al. (2004) reported that causes of EMS employee line-of-duty fatalities from 1998 to 2001 were due to aircraft accidents (57 percent, primarily from rescue helicopter crashes), motor vehicle accidents (26 percent), heart attacks/stress (7 percent), and other (11 percent).

Injuries and fatalities are not limited to employees. Students and trainees are similarly affected. Cone and McNamara (1997) surveyed emergency medicine residency programs and concluded, "Injuries sustained by [emergency medical residents in the field] during EMS rotations are uncommon but nontrivial, with several serious injuries and one fatality reported."

The problem of assaults on EMS responders has been receiving increasing attention. Mechem et al. (2002) analyzed an occupational injury database at the Philadelphia Fire Department (PFD) and found that 4 percent of occupational injuries were due to assaults. Among 1,100 employee injury reports from 1996 to 1998, the authors identified 35 involving assaults on paramedics and an additional nine involving assaults on firefighters. Forty-one percent of the assaults occurred during patient care activities, and in 82 percent of the cases, the employee

Promoting Ambulance Safety

Ambulance safety advocates recommend a multi-tiered approach to addressing the high EMS responder vehicle-related injury and death rates. The following are some examples:

One specialist advocates an interdisciplinary approach including better access to EMS accident and injury statistics, increased application of automotive safety principles to ambulance design, wearing helmets in the back of an ambulance (until other safety features are implemented), driver feedback with "black box" technology, incorporating Intelligent Transportation System technology into ambulances, consideration of ergonomics in crashworthiness research, improvements in fleet management/policy, and relevant standards to guide these processes (Levick, 2006; EMS Insider, 2006).

Green, et al. (2005) conducted computer modeling and crash testing to identify potential solutions to the high EMS employee injury rate and found opportunities for improvements in ambulance restraints, seat design, cabin geometry, and padding.

Ambulance safety is advanced by recent publications, such as the U.S. Fire Administration's Policies and Procedures for Emergency Vehicle Safety, which includes a customizable model policy (USFA/IAFC, 2006) and the American National Standards Institute's ANSI/ASSE Z15.1 standard on Safe Practices for Motor Vehicle Operators (ANSI/ASSE, 2006).

sought medical treatment. Twenty-six (59 percent) of the assaults were classified as intentional and 17 (38 percent) were considered unintentional (defined as "patient in an altered mental status"). "The finding that far more paramedics than firefighters were assaulted is noteworthy, given that at the time the PFD employed almost ten times as many firefighters as paramedics." The same authors reviewed several other studies, which suggested similar trends: 61 to 90 percent of EMS providers had been the victim of abuse or a violent act, or been assaulted on the job, usually by a patient, a patient's family member, or a bystander.

Despite the levels of assault, when Mock et al. (1999) studied the effects of violence and shift schedules on EMS providers, results suggested that the providers were no more anxious than the general working public. Cydulka et al. (1997), however, found that stress levels were "very high" among

the 22 percent of the National Association of Emergency Medical Technicians (NAEMT) membership who returned a survey, which had been sent to all members. These authors cited a number of reasons ranging from job dissatisfaction to personnel shortages.

EMS responders are also subject to bloodborne pathogen exposures. Needlesticks and other percutaneous injuries resulting in exposure to blood or other potentially infectious materials are a concern due to the high frequency of their occurrence and the potential severity of the health effects associated with exposure. When these injuries involve exposure to infectious agents, affected EMS responders are at risk of contracting disease. Exposed individuals may also suffer from adverse side effects of drugs used for post-exposure prophylaxis and from psychological stress due to the threat of infection following an exposure incident (OSHA, 2001-BBP Preamble). Surprisingly, there is some evidence that EMS responders' rate of zero-conversion for the hepatitis C virus (HCV), due to needlesticks, is similar to that of the general population. The authors hypothesize that this is a combination of the "healthy worker syndrome" (i.e., unhealthy employees leaving the profession), plus some level of increased risk due to activities associated with the EMS responder profession (compared to the general population), resulting in a neutral risk ratio (Boal et al., 2004). A separate study reported that needlestick rates were lower for EMS personnel using self-retracting lancets than other types (Peate, 2001).

These studies show the breadth of risks that EMS responders face in the line of duty. These personnel are exposed to substantial hazards from motor vehicle crashes, sprains and strains, on-the-job violence, and other significant sources of injury and illness. Comprehensive efforts to improve the occupational health and safety of EMS responders must address these factors, but should also promote adequate preparation for hazardous substance scenarios.

Appendix P

A multitude of EMS industry characteristics affect how employers make decisions about training and protecting EMS responders.

Characteristics of the EMS Industry

- The array of regulatory organizations with jurisdiction over EMS responders and the agencies for which they work.
- The diversity of state-specific certification, training, and regulatory requirements and the applicability of OSHA's HAZWOPER standard (or the equivalent in State plan states) to EMS agencies.
- The overlap between career and volunteer EMS providers.
- The overlap between public and private ambulance agencies.
- The overlap between inter-facility transporting ambulance services and emergency response services.
- The mechanism and sources used to fund EMS and the extent of such funding.
- The unique paradigms under which EMS agencies operate in order to accomplish their important public health and emergency medicine missions.
- The mutual aid agreements between EMS agencies and other organizations/jurisdictions.
- The influence of ad hoc in-the-field decisions on EMS responder health and safety.
- The employer's and contracting municipality's diligence in complying with OSHA or state health and safety regulations.
- The close relationship between this industry and hospital-based emergency services, fire departments, and hazardous materials response teams.
- The role EMS agencies play in 9-1-1 response.
- The local community's expectations regarding EMS.
- The diverse conditions under which EMS responders could work.
- The "terms of art" unique to this and closely related industries.
- The need to make informed decisions quickly based on initial information that may be incomplete.
- The limited equipment/storage space available on an ambulance.
- The challenges of treating patients while ensuring personal safety and health.

This appendix examines three specific strengths and challenges faced by the EMS industry including its relationship with the U.S. Department of Transportation's (DOT) National Highway Traffic Safety Administration (NHTSA); the applicability of federal and state OSHA HAZWOPER standards and other regulations; and the complexity created by overlapping organizational demographics of EMS responders has on the industry. Although state and federal government organizations play a large role, local EMS provider demographics also can affect the way employers implement EMS responder health and safety programs.

The Roles of NHTSA and States

NHTSA develops the National Standard Curriculum (NSC), which is voluntarily adopted by the states to meet their individual needs. States then license EMS responders and provide oversight of initial and ongoing training requirements. Typically, an EMS responder who is properly trained to the NSC, is evaluated to be competent, and meets other state requirements, is then eligible to be licensed by the state to practice.

NHTSA's NSC provides the framework for a nationally recommended minimum standard for EMS responder education. The curricula may be supplemented by additional resources and education, some of which are also available as training course outlines from NHTSA. NHTSA does not, however, dictate the amount of time trainers in a state will spend instructing on a given topic. Although objective and didactic material in the NSC contain most of the elements of OSHA's standard on Hazardous Waste Operations and Emergency Response (HAZWOPER) training, the material does not meet the requirements for HAZWOPER training. Specifically, to meet HAZWOPER requirements, the standard curricula would need to be customized to (1) include information relevant to local community conditions and (2) provide students with adequate training time to meet the HAZWOPER training requirements (e.g., 8 hours for operations level training). As a national program the NSC does not include information on specific local community conditions, nor does it specify training time requirements for those elements that could serve as the basis for meeting the general HAZWOPER training requirements.

The current EMS education system has limitations. According to an advisory panel, a more formal national EMS training program could provide

greater consistency across the U.S. (NHTSA, 2000). The advisory panel listed hazardous materials incidents as one of 22 core content categories, although compatibility with HAZWOPER training requirements is not specifically listed as an objective. A revised system, called the National EMS Education Standards is currently under development. The new system is expected to offer a more structured core content and credentialing process that will also be easier to adapt as the need arises.

The U.S. is not alone in updating EMS training standards and considering competency of EMS personnel who could respond to a hazardous material release. An EMS training system in Canada, implemented by the Minister of Health and Long-term Care in the Province of Ontario, Canada, is already incorporating a high degree of standardization into the province-wide standards for EMS training, vehicles, and equipment. While this structure might not be practical in the U.S., certain aspects may serve as illustrative examples when EMS decision makers review local, regional, state, and federal standards. In particular, since the events of September 11, 2001, policies dictate that "when an incident involves the response to hazardous materials... the expectation is that all municipal and community response agencies (fire, police, and emergency medical services) throughout the province have the capacity to respond... in keeping with the awareness level as defined by the National Fire Protection Association Standard 472 (NFPA 472): Standard for Professional Competence of Responders to Hazardous Materials Incidents (2002, Edition). This means that all responders should be able to recognize the presence of hazardous materials and take appropriate safety precautions, secure the scene of the incident, and call the appropriate authorities for assistance." (Barg, 2004).

Applicability of Federal and State OSHA HAZWOPER Standards and Other Regulations

Emergency responders at the site of a hazardous substance release are covered under OSHA's HAZWOPER standard, or the parallel OSHA-approved State Plan standard.[44] Emergency responders, including firefighters, law enforcement, and EMS personnel, are often employees of local, municipal, or state governments or effectively acting in that capacity under a contract or other agreement.

Although Federal OSHA's standards and enforcement authority do not extend to such state and local governments, these employers and employees are covered by the 26 states that operate OSHA-approved State Plans and, in states without State Plans, by the U.S. Environmental Protection Agency (EPA) with regard to HAZWOPER (29 CFR 1910.120).[45]

State Plan programs set and enforce standards, such as those for HAZWOPER and Respiratory Protection, which are identical to or "at least as effective as" Federal OSHA standards, and, therefore, may have more stringent or supplemental requirements. State Plan standards apply to state and local government employees and, in some cases, to volunteers. EPA's HAZWOPER parallel standard was adopted to cover public sector employees in states without OSHA-approved State Plans who otherwise would not be covered by the Federal OSHA standard, including volunteers who work for a government agency engaged in emergency response, such as firefighters. For consistency, OSHA interprets the HAZWOPER standard for EPA. Federal OSHA administers the safety and health program for the private sector in the remaining states and territories, and also retains authority with regard to safety and health conditions for Federal employees throughout the nation (OSHA, 1991-Borwegen).

Employers of EMS responders are also regulated under numerous and diverse local programs. Narad (1998) conducted an inventory of ambulance service regulatory programs in California and noted that "California has a variety of regulatory programs for ambulance services; these are shared among the state, county, and city governments, as well as multi-county agencies. The types of regulatory programs and the standards used vary widely around the state." This pattern is duplicated to some degree in each of the 50 states across the U.S. Although it is beyond the scope of this document to discuss individual local programs, employers need to be aware of them and communicate with local program administrators to address any conflicts between local programs and state or federal requirements.

The Influence of Overlapping Organizational Demographics of EMS Responders

One method of describing EMS responder activities is to divide them according to functional roles (those who respond to emergencies and those who

---

[44] In a letter of interpretation OSHA explained that public employee EMTs in State Plan programs must be covered by approved state OSHA standards. The extent to which volunteers are covered in State Plan programs depends on state law and policy (OSHA, 1996 – Grassley).

[45] In states without OSHA-approved State Plans, state and local government employees are covered with regards to HAZWOPER under EPA's 40 CFR Part 311.

do not). Other divisions can be made according to the type of organization the EMS responder works for, how many hours per week the responder works, or whether the responder is a volunteer.

Many EMS responders are considered "inter-facility transporting EMS responders" and primarily transfer patients to and from medical facilities under non-emergency conditions. Many of these EMS responders do not respond to 9-1-1 calls as a regular part of their jobs. In contrast, most of the remaining EMS responders do work in an emergency-response capacity at least some of the time. These two EMS responder groups have substantially different risk of encountering a hazardous substance during their normal duties.

EMS responders can be further subdivided into (1) EMS personnel for whom providing medical care before the patient arrives at a healthcare facility is the primary duty and (2) EMS responders who are cross-trained as firefighters, hazardous materials team members, or law enforcement officers.[46] In the latter case, the EMS responders' medical duties supplement the other related profession. EMS responders in both groups might experience similar ranges of hazards while performing medical care (regardless of what hazards they might encounter when filling the other role(s) for which they are cross-trained). Among fire-based EMS responders, "the integration with firefighters and associated emphasis on safety and access to quality equipment may lead to fire-based EMS systems experiencing fewer shortcomings in their [PPE] options" (LaTourrette et al., 2003).

The cross-trained EMS responders may have additional training and qualifications (e.g., to wear a higher level of respiratory protection) than EMS responders who perform only medical response activities. Those additional qualifications are related to requirements of the EMS responders' other occupational expectations and are not a traditional standard requirement for medical emergency response activities.

EMS responders may work for public, private, or contract agencies, fire departments, hospitals, or other types of organizations. This makes it difficult to fully characterize the EMS industry and has implications for how OSHA and EPA regulations are applied.

Finally, EMS responders may work full-time or part-time, or they may work on a strictly voluntary basis. An undefined number of EMS responders maintain their certification, but do not actually practice (i.e., they work in a different field).

In summary, EMS responders are a diverse group. Their risks vary with their primary and secondary roles. OSHA recognizes that this diversity of roles and risks must be taken into consideration when identifying best practices and recommendations. Additionally, state and local jurisdictions have a good deal of freedom to tailor programs to local needs; however, the number and variability of local influences affecting an individual EMS responder agency can lead to numerous requirements which are sometimes confusing.

---

[46] Approximately "40 percent of EMS response is provided by fire departments (after Karter, 2001), with independent agencies and, to a smaller extent, hospitals, private firms, and law enforcement agencies making up the remaining 60 percent." (LaTourrette et al., 2003).

OSHA®
Occupational Safety and
Health Administration

Appendix Q

Sources of Help in Addressing Biological Agent Issues

Hazardous substance release events could include the immediately identified (or announced) release of biological agents. When the hazard assessment suggests that hazardous substance releases in the region could involve biological agents, employers of EMS responders should plan to protect their workers from these agents.

Biological agents generally occur in the form of viruses, bacteria, and substances produced by biological agents (e.g., ricin). Some are infectious agents, while others cause health effects through other processes, such as toxicity. In the event that the biological agent is a viral variant with a high patient mortality rate (e.g., a pandemic influenza), EMS responders should assume (until confirmed otherwise) that the virus is spread by airborne transmission (i.e., as an aerosol) as well as by droplets. EMS responders will require respiratory protection (minimum N95).[46] This level of respiratory protection is also appropriate for bacteriological agents such as tuberculosis (TB), commonly spread by infectious process.

OSHA's standard on bloodborne pathogens (29 CFR 1910.1030) sets forth requirements for protecting workers, including EMS responders, from this type of biological agent (e.g., Hepatitis B).

More detailed information on addressing the issues surrounding biological agent exposures and disease spread by infectious processes are available at the following sources:

- Pandemic flu: www.pandemicflu.gov

- Preparing for a Bioterrorist Attack: Legal and Administrative Strategies: www.cdc.gov/ncidod/eid/vol9no2/02-0538.htm

- CDC Disease Listings (look up general and technical information on disease agents [infectious and otherwise] from anthrax to yersiniosis): www.cdc.gov/ncidod/dbmd/diseaseinfo/default.htm

- OSHA's Pandemic Influenza Preparedness and Response Guidance for Healthcare Workers and Healthcare Employers: www.osha.gov/Publications/OSHA_pandemic_health.pdf

- OSHA Regulations: Bloodborne Pathogens standard (29 CFR 1910.1030): www.osha.gov/pls/oshaweb/owadisp.show_document?p_table=STANDARDS&p_id=10051

- NIOSH page on Eye Protection for Infection Control: www.cdc.gov/niosh/topics/eye/eye-infectious.html

- CDC Infection Control Guidelines: www.cdc.gov/ncidod/dhqp/guidelines.html

- OSHA Safety and Health Topics page on possible hazards and solutions for healthcare workers at healthcare facilities and elsewhere (includes information relevant to EMS responders): www.osha.gov/SLTC/healthcarefacilities/recognition.html

- OSHA Safety and Health Topics page for Emergency Responders: www.osha.gov/SLTC/emergencypreparedness/responder.html#First

- NIOSH guidelines for healthcare workers and healthcare facilities: www.cdc.gov/niosh/hcwold0.html

- CDC Emergency Response and Preparedness page on ricin: http://www.bt.cdc.gov/agent/ricin

Concern about Needlesticks and Biological Agents

Needlesticks are one of the greatest sources of concern for EMS responders under normal conditions and the need for concern is potentially even greater during incidents involving biological agents. In the course of their job duties, EMS responders are potentially subject to exposure to blood and other potentially infectious material (OPIM). This increases their risk of exposure to bloodborne diseases, such as hepatitis B and C and human immunodeficiency virus (HIV) (Adams & Elliot, 2006; Boal et al., 2005; Peate, 2001; Rischitelli et al., 2001). EMS responders are also exposed to airborne infectious diseases, like meningococcal meningitis and tuberculosis which have serious health effects (Miller et al., 2005). Exposed individuals may also suffer from adverse side effects of drugs used for post-exposure prophylaxis and from psychological stress due to the threat of infection following an exposure incident (OSHA, 2001-BBP Preamble). Because EMS

---

[46] Airborne transmission, as occurs in tuberculosis, is spread through small infectious particles such as droplet nuclei. Unlike the larger droplets, these very small airborne droplet nuclei can be readily disseminated by air currents to susceptible individuals. They can travel significant distances and can penetrate deep into the lung to the alveoli where they can establish an infection. The presence of significant airborne transmission would indicate the need for ventilation procedures and respiratory protection greater than that afforded by a surgical mask, e.g., a NIOSH-certified N95 or higher respirator.

responder work is performed in uncontrolled, emergency environments, usually dealing with trauma or sudden onset of illness, there is a greater potential for needlesticks or blood exposure to occur (Boal et al., 2005; Peate, 2001).

Preliminary results of a national study to prevent blood exposure in paramedics by the Pennsylvania Department of Health determined that blood exposures occurred through (1) needle or lancet stick, (2) cuts from sharp objects, (3) blood in eyes, nose or mouth, (4) uncooperative or combative patient bites (skin break) and (5) blood on non-intact skin (Pennsylvania Department of Health, 2007). Twenty-two percent of the paramedics reported at least one exposure to blood and an additional seven percent reported more than one blood exposure in the last twelve months of service (Pennsylvania Department of Health, 2007).

EMS responders do not always report the exposure. The Pennsylvania study cited reasons for non-report as:

- The paramedic did not consider the exposure significant or forgot about the exposure.
- The paramedic determined that he/she was too busy and reporting involved too much paperwork.
- The paramedic did not want to be reprimanded.
- The paramedic was worried that somebody would find out about the exposure.
- The paramedic thought that the company rarely took action when a worker is exposed.

The critical concept in this kind of responder work is the need to focus on prevention of exposure to blood and OPIM (Boal et al., 2005). A review of literature determined that combinations of strategies reduced needlestick injuries for healthcare employees. Enhanced training on sharps education, safe needle choice, a uniform approach to exposure plans with concise treatment protocol, and limiting long work hours have been cited as actions that decrease needlestick injuries (Adams & Elliot, 2006; Ilhan et al., 2006; Miller et al., 2005; Peate, 2001).

OSHA Assistance

OSHA can provide extensive help through a variety of programs, including technical assistance about effective safety and health programs, state plans, workplace consultations, and training and education.

Effective management of worker safety and health protection is a decisive factor in reducing the extent and severity of work-related injuries and illnesses and their related costs. In fact, an effective safety and health management system forms the basis of good worker protection, can save time and money, increase productivity and reduce employee injuries, illnesses and related workers' compensation costs.

To assist employers and workers in developing effective safety and health management systems, OSHA published recommended Safety and Health Program Management Guidelines (54 *Federal Register* (16): 3904-3916, January 26, 1989). These voluntary guidelines can be applied to all places of employment covered by OSHA.

The guidelines identify four general elements critical to the development of a successful safety and health management system:

* Management leadership and worker involvement,
* Worksite analysis,
* Hazard prevention and control, and
* Safety and health training.

The guidelines recommend specific actions, under each of these general elements, to achieve an effective safety and health management system. The *Federal Register* notice is available online at www.osha.gov.

State Programs

The *Occupational Safety and Health Act of 1970* (OSH Act) encourages states to develop and operate their own job safety and health plans. OSHA approves and monitors these plans. Twenty-five states, Puerto Rico and the Virgin Islands currently operate approved state plans: 22 cover both private and public (state and local government) employment; Connecticut, Illinois, New Jersey, New York and the Virgin Islands cover the public sector only. States and territories with their own OSHA-approved occupational safety and health plans must adopt standards identical to, or at least as effective as, the Federal OSHA standards.

Consultation Services

Consultation assistance is available on request to employers who want help in establishing and maintaining a safe and healthful workplace. Largely funded by OSHA, the service is provided at no cost to the employer. Primarily developed for smaller employers with more hazardous operations, the consultation service is delivered by state governments employing professional safety and health consultants. Comprehensive assistance includes an appraisal of all mechanical systems, work practices and occupational safety and health hazards of the workplace and all aspects of the employer's present job safety and health program. In addition, the service offers assistance to employers in developing and implementing an effective safety and health program. No penalties are proposed or citations issued for hazards identified by the consultant. OSHA provides consultation assistance to the employer with the assurance that his or her name and firm and any information about the workplace will not be routinely reported to OSHA enforcement staff. For more information concerning consultation assistance, see OSHA's website at www.osha.gov.

Strategic Partnership Program

OSHA's Strategic Partnership Program helps encourage, assist and recognize the efforts of partners to eliminate serious workplace hazards and achieve a high level of worker safety and health. Most strategic partnerships seek to have a broad impact by building cooperative relationships with groups of employers and workers. These partnerships are voluntary relationships between OSHA, employers, worker representatives, and others (e.g., trade unions, trade and professional associations, universities, and other government agencies).

For more information on this and other agency programs, contact your nearest OSHA office, or visit OSHA's website at www.osha.gov.

OSHA Training and Education

OSHA area offices offer a variety of information services, such as technical advice, publications, audiovisual aids and speakers for special engagements. OSHA's Training Institute in Arlington Heights, IL, provides basic and advanced courses in safety and health for Federal and state compliance officers, state consultants, Federal agency personnel, and private sector employers, workers and their representatives.

The OSHA Training Institute also has established OSHA Training Institute Education Centers to address the increased demand for its courses from the private sector and from other federal agencies. These centers are colleges, universities and nonprofit organizations that have been selected after a competition for participation in the program.

OSHA also provides funds to nonprofit organizations, through grants, to conduct workplace training and education in subjects where OSHA believes there is a lack of workplace training. Grants are awarded annually.

For more information on grants, training and education, contact the OSHA Training Institute, Directorate of Training and Education, 2020 South Arlington Heights Road, Arlington Heights, IL 60005, (847) 297-4810, or see Training on OSHA's website at www.osha.gov. For further information on any OSHA program, contact your nearest OSHA regional office listed at the end of this publication.

Information Available Electronically

OSHA has a variety of materials and tools available on its website at www.osha.gov. These include electronic tools, such as *Safety and Health Topics, eTools, Expert Advisors*; regulations, directives and publications; videos and other information for employers and workers. OSHA's software programs and eTools walk you through challenging safety and health issues and common problems to find the best solutions for your workplace.

OSHA Publications

OSHA has an extensive publications program. For a listing of free items, visit OSHA's website at www.osha.gov or contact the OSHA Publications Office, U.S. Department of Labor, 200 Constitution Avenue, NW, N-3101, Washington, DC 20210; telephone (202) 693-1888 or fax to (202) 693-2498.

Contacting OSHA

To report an emergency, file a complaint, or seek OSHA advice, assistance, or products, call (800) 321-OSHA or contact your nearest OSHA Regional or Area office listed at the end of this publication. The teletypewriter (TTY) number is (877) 889-5627.

Written correspondence can be mailed to the nearest OSHA Regional or Area Office listed at the end of this publication or to OSHA's national office at: U.S. Department of Labor, Occupational Safety and Health Administration, 200 Constitution Avenue, N.W., Washington, DC 20210.

By visiting OSHA's website at www.osha.gov, you can also:
- File a complaint online,
- Submit general inquiries about workplace safety and health electronically, and
- Find more information about OSHA and occupational safety and health.

Occupational Safety and Health Administration

OSHA Regional Offices

Region I
(CT*, ME, MA, NH, RI, VT*)
JFK Federal Building, Room E340
Boston, MA 02203
(617) 565-9860

Region II
(NJ*, NY*, PR*, VI*)
201 Varick Street, Room 670
New York, NY 10014
(212) 337-2378

Region III
(DE, DC, MD*, PA, VA*, WV)
The Curtis Center
170 S. Independence Mall West
Suite 740 West
Philadelphia, PA 19106-3309
(215) 861-4900

Region IV
(AL, FL, GA, KY*, MS, NC*, SC*, TN*)
61 Forsyth Street, SW, Room 6T50
Atlanta, GA 30303
(404) 562-2300

Region V
(IL*, IN*, MI*, MN*, OH, WI)
230 South Dearborn Street
Room 3244
Chicago, IL 60604
(312) 353-2220

Region VI
(AR, LA, NM*, OK, TX)
525 Griffin Street, Room 602
Dallas, TX 75202
(972) 850-4145

Region VII
(IA*, KS, MO, NE)
Two Pershing Square
2300 Main Street, Suite 1010
Kansas City, MO 64108-2416
(816) 283-8745

Region VIII
(CO, MT, ND, SD, UT*, WY*)
1999 Broadway, Suite 1690
PO Box 46550
Denver, CO 80202-5716
(720) 264-6550

Region IX
(AZ*, CA*, HI*, NV*, and American Samoa,
Guam and the Northern Mariana Islands)
90 7th Street, Suite 18-100
San Francisco, CA 94103
(415) 625-2547

Region X
(AK*, ID, OR*, WA*)
1111 Third Avenue, Suite 715
Seattle, WA 98101-3212
(206) 553-5930

* These states and territories operate their own OSHA-approved job safety and health programs and cover state and local government employees as well as private sector employees. The Connecticut, Illinois, New Jersey, New York and Virgin Islands plans cover public employees only. States with approved programs must have standards that are identical to, or at least as effective as, the Federal OSHA standards.

Note: To get contact information for OSHA Area Offices, OSHA-approved State Plans and OSHA Consultation Projects, please visit us online at www.osha.gov or call us at 1-800-321-OSHA.